CW00419308

FIFTY YEARS IN THE YORKSHIRE DALES

FIFTY YEARS
in the
YORKSHIRE DALES

By MARIE HARTLEY
and JOAN INGILBY

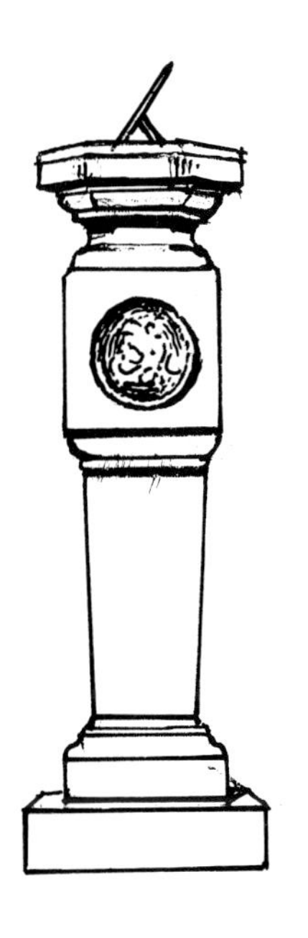

SMITH SETTLE

First published in 1995 by
Smith Settle Ltd
Ilkley Road
Otley
Wset Yorkshire
LS21 3JP

ISBN Paperback 1 85825 052 8
ISBN Hardback 1 85825 053 6

British Library Cataloguing-in-Publication data:
A catalogue record for this book is available from the British Library.

Set in Monotype Garamond

Designed, printed and bound by
SMITH SETTLE
Ilkley Road, Otley, West Yorkshire LS21 3JP

Contents

List of Illustrations vii
Photographic Acknowledgements ix
Preface xi

A New Partnership 1
Background to Work 9
A Lasting Friendship 16
Yorkshire Village 24
The Yorkshire Dales 34
In the Public Eye 45
A Famous Guest 51
Askrigg Art Club 56
A Trio of Books 62
Life and Tradition in the Yorkshire Dales 72
Life and Tradition in the Moorlands of North-East Yorkshire 81
Life and Tradition in West Yorkshire 92
A Decade of Achievement 101
Two Albums 112
A Summing Up 120

Publications 131

List of Illustrations

Marie Hartley and Joan Ingilby at work, 1948 3
Grandmothers' Treasures exhibition at the York Festival in 1951 5
Ella Pontefract, 1935 6
Ella in London in 1931 7
Aldine House, Dent's offices 8
Dick Chapman fishing 9
Allan and Rosalie Hartley and their children 11
Portrait of Dorothy Una Ratcliffe 12
George Jackson 13
Fred Lawson 13
Phyllis Bentley at her desk 17
Ring of Brognar, Orkney 22
Viking longhouse, Birsay, Orkney 22
Joan and Phyllis on the Isle of Man 23
Wren Library, Trinity College, Cambridge 27
Askrigg from Coleshouse garden 30
Askrigg from Abbey Heads 31
Askrigg main street in winter 31
Crummackdale 35
Deepdale 38
Gunnerside 39
Joan and Phyllis at the top of the Eiffel Tower 42
Four crayon drawings of Paris by Marie 43
Marie and Joan at a literary luncheon 45
Semerwater in winter 46
Smoke over Askrigg village 47
W T Oliver 48
J B Priestley painting at Ribblehead 51
Hubberholme, where J B's ashes are scattered 55
Askrigg Art Club evening class 58
Art Club Christmas party 59
Askrigg Art Club annual outing 60
Marie and Joan in the new room 62
Vale of York from Sutton Bank 65
Marie and Joan sitting under the cherry tree 67
Cricket Hill, Bennington College, Vermont 73
The Ukraine, Moscow 73
Dentdale 76
Swaledale sheep waiting to be fed 77

Bert Frank with a corn dolly 81
Raymond Hayes 82
Major and Mrs J Fairfax-Blakeborough 83
Thatching at the Ryedale Folk Museum 84
Hanging pictures at the 1979 Askrigg Produce Show 85
Joan Ingilby, president of the Askrigg Produce Show 85
Marie and Joan in their vegetable garden 88
Joan feeding the hens 88
Harvesting in Farndale 89
Hebden Bridge 93
Heights of the Calder Valley 96
Dean Clough Mills, Halifax 96
Brodsworth Colliery 97
Setting up the museum in March 1979 102
Opening of the Upper Dales Folk Museum 102
Friends of the Museum visiting Jervaulx Abbey 103
Garden party at Coleshouse 104
Outing of the Friends to Burtersett Quarries 105
Exhibition of our work at Askrigg in 1972 106
Guided tour of Askrigg 107
Handing over the manuscript of *Dales Memories* 110
Joan, Bill Mitchell and Marie 110
Degree ceremony at the University of York 112
Signing copies of *Yorkshire Album* 116
George and Mary Ellison, Dentdale 117
William and Mary Mason of Appletreewick 117
Florence and Frank Carr, with Joan 117
Marie at work on a wood engraving 120
Brian Settle and Ken Smith 121
Anne and Fred Burkhardt and family 123
Marie and Joan undertaking fieldwork 124
The exhibition 'Forms and Colours with Documents' 125
Retrospective exhibition at Ingleton, 1993 126
Joan and Marie at the exhibition at the Leeds University Gallery 127
Silver Medal presentation at the Yorkshire Archaeological Society 128
Marie and Joan respond 128

Photographic Acknowledgements

The following photographs on the pages listed are reproduced by courtesy of the following:

B. Unné, 3; Leeds City Art Gallery, 12; R B Fawcett, 13; W H Womersley, 13; the Master and Fellows of Trinity College Cambridge, 27; The *Yorkshire Post*, 48, 81 The *Yorkshire Evening Post*, 121; Mark Gerson, 62; D S Hall, 88; A Burkhardt, 73; J C Moore, 102; A Meadows, 106; A Holubecki, 105, 124, 126; E Burgin, 107, 125, 127; M Farnell, 120; J Telford, 128.

Apart from a few photographs whose origin we do not know, the remainder of the photographs are by the authors.

Fond memory brings the light
Of other days around me

T Moore

Preface

On 22nd August 1991, it was suggested by letter from Ken Smith of Smith Settle Ltd, printers and publishers based at Otley, that we write an account of the lives and work of Ella Pontefract and ourselves to be published in 1994. As we were engaged on other books at the time, we do not remember registering a great deal of interest. But the idea must have germinated in our minds, and in the autumn of 1994 we began work on our reminiscences in earnest. We have felt unable to include Ella because Marie had written *Yorkshire Heritage*, a tribute to her following her death in 1945, published by Dent. This gave biographical details from Ella's childhood onwards and the full story of the Pontefract/Hartley partnership, which resulted in the pioneer three Dales books, *Swaledale, Wensleydale* and *Wharfedale* of the 1930s, *The Charm of Yorkshire Churches, Yorkshire Tour* and *Yorkshire Cottage*. To start all over again on those days would have been repetitive, so in effect this book, beginning in 1947, is a sequel to *Yorkshire Heritage*.

Fifty Years in the Yorkshire Dales records the work of the Hartley/Ingilby partnership, which began when Joan joined Marie in 1947 to continue work on Yorkshire and the Dales. It is based partially on memory, but also on the diaries, notes for the books, and letters from publishers and readers, which we have preserved assiduously. It has to be said that the diaries sometimes fail us, neglected when we were pressed for time. But we have been able to give, as it were, a blow-by-blow account of how we wrote the books, nineteen altogether counting Marie's art books and Joan's poems.

One chapter puts on record the sixteen enjoyable years of the Askrigg Art Club — a hobby to which we gave time freely and of which we are proud, for it offered many people a new vision and an outlet for their talents. A few chapters relate to friends, famous and otherwise, who chanced to come our way. In our relationship with the Dales people we have been trusted, and have made many many friends. It has been of concern to us that we have not always had time to keep up with some who helped and with whom we formed happy relationships. We could not have worked among more co-operative and courteous people, and we remember with pleasure the many times we have been greeted with welcoming smiles — never a sour note of any moment. Goodwill, which we prize, has been our lot.

Similarly, in other parts of Yorkshire we have met kindly people and have made many friends. (Sometimes watching television, with its emphasis all too often on the depraved, we cannot believe that we live in the same world.) Our happy recollections of the moorlands of north-east Yorkshire and of the years spent in West Yorkshire will hold fast in our minds for as long as we live.

Sometimes in this age of emphasis on 'Feminism' we wonder whether we have suffered in our work by being women. It is obvious that in general the status of women has improved throughout our lifetimes. But we have come to the conclusion that it has not mattered. A little fame has brought us respect.

Like many elderly people, we look back on the past in the Dales with nostalgia. Today it is in some ways a different world. On the whole the landscape, preserved by the officers of the Yorkshire Dales National Park, is unspoilt, except that flowery meadows are rare, barns in jeopardy, and rows of black plastic bags are spewed out by modern haymaking methods. As do many other people, we approve of the Park and its authority, with the proviso that occasionally some of its planning decisions are arbitrary and deplorable. (In its early days Marie was on the commitee of the Park, and wrote the first leaflet about the region. But she is not a committee person, and was relieved to resign.)

The real change is that the working community of farmers (not always in good economic shape, as witnessed in the slump of the 1930s), ancillary trades and professions has had implanted on it all the trappings of a holiday resort, with its influx of visitors, new residents and facilities to go with them. Although visitors are by no means a modern phenomenon, the numbers are. Possibly the development is a rescue bid for the future prosperity of the region. We look back with gratitude for our sojourn in this beautiful place.

MH & JI 1995

A NEW PARTNERSHIP

In 1947, following the death of Ella Pontefract two years earlier, Joan Ingilby chose to join Marie Hartley at Askrigg to form a new partnership. She had been a friend for several years, and family circumstances — her father's ill-health and removal to a warmer climate — led to the decision. The question arose what were we to start on. Our friend, E F Bozman (who was known as Bozzie) of J M Dent & Son, who had published the Pontefract/ Hartley books, had been deeply saddened by Ella's death, and he assumed that as she was the writer, there would be no more manuscripts. But as time went on, Marie formed the wish to write a memoir to Ella describing their travels, research and publications, and in December 1947, Dents signalled approval of such a book.

However, our first joint venture was to embark on contributions for magazines, which began in 1947 with articles for *Yorkshire Advertiser* and *Yorkshire Illustrated.* In early March 1948, we explored and took photographs of lead-mining sites in Swaledale. We well remember the enjoyment of those days out at Old Gang, Hurst, Marrick and Swinnergill, enlivened by talks with the Dalesfolk we met on the way. We submitted 'Lead-mining Country' to *Country Life*, and were delighted to receive a letter from the editor accepting it. Other articles followed in that magazine over the years, and also reviews of our books, for the editor, John Adams, was a Yorkshireman interested in our work.

In March 1948, Harry Scott, the founder and editor of the *Yorkshire Dalesman*, as it was then called, had written as follows: 'I wondered if you and Miss Ingilby would care to consider the preparation of a Dalesman Pocket Book on the old Dent knitting industry ... The length of such an MS should be about 12,000 words and would of course entail some research and enquiry on the spot if it was to be authoritative'. As this was a commission on a subject which we welcomed, and would not take too long, the memoir was temporarily shelved. The project was to become *The Old Hand-Knitters of the Dales*, published in 1951, one of the most rewarding and enjoyable of our undertakings.

It is worth recording that Ella and Marie had generously supported Harry Scott in his pioneer effort to establish a new magazine which was eventually to be called the *Dalesman.* When in 1939 its success was threatened by the outbreak of war, and its fate hung in the balance, Harry Scott wrote: 'To both of these groups (dalesfolk and visitors) I feel you have contributed so greatly that any success the magazine achieved will be in a large part due to you'. Sometimes we used to think of Mr Scott as rather tough, but now reading the letters fifty years on, we are struck by their warmth and friendliness.

In 1948 we found that very little work had been done on either knitting in general or knitting as a branch of the textile industry in the Dales and elsewhere. It was inclined to be thought of as a hobby entirely for women. Also the emphasis on Dent, because of the well-known phrase 'the terrible knitters e' Dent', obscured its importance to the economy of the Dales in general (second only to lead-mining). (Ella and Marie had pointed out the prominence of the industry in Wensleydale in the book of that name in 1936.) In competition with machine knitting, hand-knitting as an industry, starting in Elizabethan times, lasted until about 1900. It survived so long largely owing to the skill of the knitters, their low pay, and the type of goods produced. So in 1948 we were just in time to collect some first-hand impressions of its later stage, when the hosier, who had been the key figure, had, following the Industrial Revolution, become the mill owner, still supplying yarn to the knitters in their homes.

We began with printed sources, and far beyond our brief compiled a first chapter on 'Knitting in Early Times', followed by a chapter on the knitting industry in general. Books were borrowed from the London Library, of which Joan was a life member. We also wrote to or visited museums from the Victoria and Albert to the many Yorkshire museums, in order to locate knitted garments or aids to knitting. The fine silk shirts at the Victoria and Albert were far removed from the utilitarian jerseys, caps and stockings from the Dales. Such goods, worn out and dispensed with, were non-existent, except for the patterned Dent gloves which had the name of the owner knitted into the wristband. When we turned to the Dales, a wealth of untapped sources were to be found in printed volumes, such as Howitt's *Rural life in England* (1844) and Adam Sedgwick's *Memorials of Cowgill Chapel* (1868), and many more. Documents were rare, but what we found, priceless. The wonderful Dover letter book was lent to us by Mr J D Betham, a nephew of the Dovers, who ran Hebblethwaite and Farfield mills near or at Sedbergh. These were so valuable that we added an appendix quoting some fifty letters verbatim. A large box of papers relating to the Flax Mill at Askrigg was a find amongst the archives of the Yorkshire Archaeological Society in Leeds, giving as it did the full story of that mill, like others sorely troubled. Members of the Gill family who ran Low Mill, Askrigg, up to 1875, were still alive, and both John and William (aged 89) described the premises, the crude machinery, the mill cat, and the journeys with 'grove yarn' for the lead-miners in Swaledale. As far as we know, no records have survived of Smith's mill at Hawes, then remembered by a few people who had worked for or at it. Another ledger from Satron mill, Swaledale, was lent to us by Mr Marmaduke Clarkson, the vet for upper Swaledale, who together with his sister we knew well. This was a corn mill, but knitting was mentioned.

It was our good fortune to meet some of the old knitters, then quite elderly. They all knitted as in ordinary knitting, but by having learnt to knit from childhood, and by using traditional aids, they attained a remarkable speed. These aids consisted basically of a knitting sheath, usually wooden, a leather belt and curved needles, one of which fitted into a hole at the top of the sheath, which itself was tucked into the belt on the right-hand side, and thus one needle was held firm. The sheaths or sticks, have become collector's items, and a specialist study of their own. (Even now in 1995 we are corresponding with a doctor who is researching these artefacts in the British Isles and Europe.)

At Dent we had friends who kept the antique shop there, and when we called the

Marie Hartley and Joan Ingilby at work in the studio, 1948, before the workroom was built.

previous owner, Mrs Agar, was staying with them. She herself had amassed a collection of over ninety sheaths, and she took us to see Mrs Sally Crabtree, who lived up Flintergill in Dent Town. We found Mrs Crabtree engaged in knitting a sock using all the traditional equipment, and she told us that as a child she knitted after returning home from school, but that her mother was a better knitter than she was. 'My mother's needles fair made music.' We also spoke to Mrs Martin of Gayle near Hawes, one of a family of thirteen, who had knitted for Smith's mill, and whose father worked there whilst her mother ran the farm. Ever-present poverty was exacerbated by large families. Another old knitter, Mrs Martha Dinsdale of Appersett, near Hawes, used to knit 'ganseys' for Smith's mill (six for 6s). 'They were fain to deu it'.

One source of information, census returns, which give occupations, were not then available. In these, knitters and woolcombers occur frequently in the returns for the hamlets round Hawes. Occupations also given are 'pauper knitters' and, for children aged from six to nine, 'Knitters and Sunday scholars'. In 1861 in Gayle there were twenty-three 'Knitters of Ruff Hosiery', and at Burtersett and Appersett 'Knitters of Guernsey Frocks'. These were huge knitted shirts, which were milled to make them waterproof, worn by sailors and fishermen outside their other clothes. Although knitters today may use a knitting sheath, they willingly admit that they cannot achieve the speed, in which the loops could scarcely be seen passing from one needle to another. It is a skill that has gone. We have since regretted that we did not borrow a ciné camera to take photographs of Mrs Crabtree 'swaving' as it was called. It has to be said that our interest lay in the industry and its participants rather than in the craft of knitting itself.

In November 1948 we posted the manuscript. It was about 27,000 words, more than twice the number originally allotted to us, but we do not remember any protests. Completion had been complicated by the death of Marie's father, bringing sadness and also disruption to our schedule. Alas, the self-employed have need to strike a balance between duty and work. However, rather to our dismay Mr Scott delayed publication until June 1951.

There were two interesting spin-offs. Mrs Curwen, the wife of a vicar of Dent who went there in 1910, sent us four pairs of Dent gloves, two adults' and two childrens', also a knitting sheath and needles belonging to a famous Dent knitter, Mary Allen, who had died in 1924. All of these treasures are now on display at the Dales Countryside Museum at Hawes. Mrs Curwen told us that in those days there were 'a good number of excellent knitters in Dent'. Many years later we visited Mary Allen's son, Canon E Allen, at Settle, and he gave us a pair of grey-blue mittens with 'God be with you' worked into the wristband, which his mother had knitted for him during the First World War.

At that time Askrigg had a Women's Institute, and from headquarters came the request to stage a knitting display at a Grandmothers' Treasures exhibition at St William's College for the first York Festival in 1951. In order to fashion a knitter we were lent a tailor's dummy, a bust and a separate head. But the bust lacked arms, and we enlisted the help of our friend, the blacksmith, who made a light iron framework with arms held in the correct position for knitting. Others lent clothes, including a long woollen skirt which hid the fact that the figure had no legs. We seated 'Granny' in a high chair in our dining-room, and many were the startled looks as friends and neighbours came in to view. Granny, surrounded by gloves, knitting sheaths, a wool winder, a spinning wheel and weights, made a striking exhibit at York.

The publication of the book aroused interest, and a large file of letters accumulated. One woman wrote to say that she had given many lectures in different parts of the country, and had quoted liberally from our book, but, she told us, not mentioning

The Grandmothers' Treasures exhibition organised by the Yorkshire Federation of Womens' Institutes at the first York Festival in 1951. Marie and Joan arranged this hand-knitting display.

our names. As time went on, the book languished out of print, and became sought after, but it was reprinted in an abridged edition in 1969, in 1978 and 1988, and in full in 1991. In 1964 we had visited Shetland and had been delighted to meet Shetlanders who knitted in the same way as the Dales' knitters had done. The Japanese, interested

Ella Pontefract, 1935.

in crafts, were brought to see us by Sue Leighton-White, a knitting specialist, and they published comprehensive articles on Dales' knitting in two glossy *Vogue*-type Japanese magazines.

Meanwhile Marie was writing the memoir to Ella Pontefract, which she mostly accomplished sitting by the fire and writing on a small table surrounded by diaries and the Pontefract/Hartley books. (We had not then built on the workroom at the back of the house.) In April 1949, a few chapters were sent to Bozzie at Dents in London, who approved them. Previously he had had to be persuaded that they were all written by Marie. The misunderstanding arose because Ella had signed a contract with Dents on 31st August 1942, to write a country book, not a history, to be called 'Yorkshire Village', but because of her ill-health only notes had been made. (It is sad to remember that no medication whatsoever was available in the mid-1940s for her complaint — high blood pressure.) By May Marie was finishing the manuscript, which Joan read through, before posting it on June 14th. Bozzie wrote appreciatively: 'I found it thoroughly readable and the tension was maintained, and altogether it makes a fine tribute to E P.'

Ella outside 11 Endsleigh Street, London, in 1931.

The illustrations had yet to be tackled. Instead of pen-and-ink Marie chose brush-and-ink, a new medium admired by many but not by everyone. As our work had covered all Yorkshire, we motored from as far afield as Holderness to the Westmorland border, often returning home late in the evening with several drawings. We supplied ten photographs, in order to include one of Ella and treasures such as that of Jane Ryder of Redmire, Wensleydale, and one lent by the Aldersons of Stone House, Keld, of two Alderson schoolchildren of about 1890 dressed in corduroy suits and wearing bowler hats. A further addition were seven two-tone full-page drawings, which eventually posed production problems.

We visited Dents in London in October, and discussed the illustrations with Bozzie and Martin Dent, head of production and grandson of the founder of the firm. Marie, who had illustrated the early books with wood engravings, was invited to attend the opening of an exhibition entitled 'Wood Engraving in Modern English books', at the headquarters of the National Book League in Albemarle Street, then a rendezvous

Aldine House, Dent's offices in Bedford Street, London.

for anyone connected with books. Bozzie introduced her to the opener, Robert Gibbings, whose books of engravings were published by Dents. Many years on Marie's engravings, as we shall see, were suddenly re-discovered.

As happened all too often in later years, trouble dogged the choice of title of the memoir, which has not seemed to be our forte. 'Far above Ure's Rills' was deemed too clumsy; 'Yorkshire Folk' was already used by someone, until 'Yorkshire Harvest' was turned into *Yorkshire Heritage.* Our files of Dent letters for this book contain forty-six letters dealing with production, the illustrations and book wrapper designed by Marie. We were even sent a sample of cloth to be used for the case to approve the colour. This was publishing in the old style with the author consulted at every turn. Good production was the hallmark of Dent books. They had their own printing press, the Aldine Press, at Letchworth, opened in 1906 by J M Dent, the founder of the firm at the time of the inauguration of their famous Everyman's Library. In 1946 labour shortages persisted from the war years. It was proposed that Ella's contract for her book, for which she had been advanced £100, should serve as Marie's with a qualifying letter, plus £50 for the illustrations.

Yorkshire Heritage was published on 31st August 1950 at 16s. It pleased Bozzie that this was well before the publication of *The Old Hand-Knitters.* On following days we visited Bradford to sign books at Brown Muff's in the morning, and Busbys in the afternoon. In those days the managers of the book departments knew us well, and took us out to lunch or tea. At Walker's bookshop in Leeds, where they had arranged a splendid window display, Marie signed books solidly for an hour and a half, and on a third day she was at Smith's in Harrogate — all heart-warming occasions. Some forty small and twelve lengthy notices in local and national papers reviewed it favourably, and the title appeared in nine advertisements of Dent's general list. (Nowadays few books, and those mostly blockbusters, are advertised.) Sales were reasonable rather than spectacular. At the time it was perhaps too recent history, whereas today the book is a valuable period piece. It did establish Marie as a writer, and so paved the way for Dents to look favourably on future work from the new partnership.

BACKGROUND TO WORK

Yorkshire Heritage was published on 31st August 1950, and on Sunday 15th October we set out to visit and discuss a new project with our friend, Dick Chapman. He was a native of Askrigg who Marie had known since 1935, a widower living with his two daughters at Bingley, and master at Saltaire Road Senior Boys School at Shipley. In 1944, together with the headmaster of Yorebridge Grammar School, R C Shorter, Dick had written a pageant based on the history of Askrigg for a wartime event called 'Salute The Soldier'. It was a memorable occasion in the annals of the village. Although six years had passed, perhaps this sparked off the idea of a village history based on Askrigg, but at the time we thought of it as a subject for a new book to start on near at hand. We enquired whether he regarded such a subject as his province and he answered 'No'. Dick helped and took a keen interest in it from start to finish, and at the end wrote, 'I've had a lot of enjoyment without the work'. We were heartened by his promise of co-operation. Goodwill is a pearl without price.

One of Dick's activities was to bring parties of his pupils, some, deprived children, to camp in Wensleydale. He also once gave us a little book, entitled 'Glen Beck', half-bound in red cloth, compiled by thirteen boys from the school, who in 1942-3 had

Dick Chapman fishing in the River Ure.

explored the beck near Saltaire, written up their findings, printed and illustrated it with linocuts. No doubt it owed much to Dick's guidance, and that of his colleague, Laurie Town, art master at the school. But it was an achievement. Town had given us two copies of *Wensleydale* bound in green leather. Dick put altruism into practice. He retired in 1955, first to Dale Grange, then Bainbridge, and, a great fisherman, he became water bailiff for a stretch of the River Ure, and was appointed an inspector of Ancient Monuments for this part of the North Riding. He remained a valued friend, and it was a moving moment when he thanked us for our friendship at the end of his life in 1981.

Before continuing with the story of the village, and lest we seem to be writing in a vacuum, the visits of relations and friends are worth recording. In those days, we spent holidays with Marie's mother at Scarborough and Joan's at Ringwood, Hampshire, and our parents came to stay with us. Journeys were long, sometimes undertaken by train, sometimes by car, in those days when traffic was light and motorways unknown. Also, at Easter, for several years Marie's brother, Allan, brought his wife and four children to stay with us. Our three bedrooms were stretched to the limit, camp beds installed, and quantities of food baked. We look back on those happy times with particular pleasure, on the walks, drives and picnics, on sitting in the garden in deckchairs in brilliant sunshine, or driven indoors by rain. Allan was a special person, kindly, gentle, musical, and concerned for his family's welfare. Although the visits continued, they were different after Allan's tragic early death in 1955.

From time to time we set out for London, and a few times drove by car from Askrigg to our hotel in Bloomsbury in order to attend meetings at Aldine House, Dent's offices, and to enjoy the theatres and art galleries of the capital.

The visitors, too, who arrived on our doorstep in 1948 to 1950 are recorded in diaries for those years, which marked the beginning of several friendships. Phyllis Bentley, who called in 1949, is given a chapter to herself later in this book. W B Crump, with whom we shared many interests, and his daughter, Barbara, came in June 1948. A name possibly nearly forgotten, he wrote pioneer works: T*he History of the Huddersfield Woollen Industry*, 1935, with Gertrude Ghorbal; *Huddersfield Highways Down the Ages*, 1949; and *The Little Hill Farm*, 1938 and 1951. The little hill farms which Mr Crump had known as a boy were round Halifax, and writing in his eighty-second year, he was able to recollect old farming methods long since abandoned. Marie had provided a drawing for the frontispiece of this book, and Ella Pontefract had reviewed the first edition in the *Yorkshire Post.*

Early in July 1949, we were preparing for the arrival of a party of thirty-two members of the Association of Yorkshire Bookmen. Later in the month our friend, John Lawrence, came to stay in the village. During the war he had been based on Catterick Camp as officer in charge of map-reading sorties all over the Dales hills. A Cambridge man, he took a personal interest in our work, and in the early days suggested general historical books to help our research. On this visit, during a walk to the top of Great Shunnor Fell he lost his wallet. Because we were tied up, the help of Dick Chapman was enlisted, and they set off up the same route as before and found it.

Allan and Rosalie Hartley and their children in the garden at Coleshouse.

Dorothy Una Ratcliffe: portrait by Ambrose McEvoy, in the City Art Gallery, Leeds.

John, education officer, first in the army and then in the RAF living at Colchester, never lost his love for the Dales, and came annually on holiday, always staying in the same rooms, until in 1994, on what would have been his fiftieth visit, he had to give up owing to ill-health. In October Harry Scott, by now editor of a well-established and successful magazine, the *Dalesman*, had tea with us before giving a lecture to the Women's Institute.

In September 1949, Dorothy Una Ratcliffe, her husband, and sister came to tea. A diary entry reads: 'D U R looked stunning, in grey corduroy'. The acquaintance dated back to the 1930s, and this was now one of recurring visits and invitations to lunches and dinners. She brought with her a copy of *Until the Dawn*, lyrics in Yorkshire dialect and standard English, inscribed for Joan Ingilby. The year before on a visit in March she had given Marie a recently-published children's book *Land of the Little Years.* A world traveller, with manifold interests, wealthy and married three times, and the writer of a great body of work, D U R related to the Dales (and elsewhere) to local folk, artists and authors, with simple pleasure. Many books flowed from her pen: a few children's, a few travel, numerous plays, and, above all, verse both in Yorkshire dialect and standard English. All were handsomely produced, and some such as *Fairings* (poems), 1928, and *Lillilows* (character sketches), 1931, were brilliantly illustrated by Fred Lawson, the artist living at Castle Bolton, Wensleydale. She also promoted magazines such as *The Northern Broadsheet*, to which we were asked to contribute.

George Jackson, artist, playwright, editor and teacher, sewing part of a costume for a play.

Her appearance was in keeping with her personality, tall and graceful; she appropriately wore a cloak that floated behind her. Her looks were handsome rather than pretty, and with high colouring her face was framed with curling brown hair. Her portrait painted by Ambrose McEvoy is more than a good likeness, tinged as it is with her aura of otherworldliness. Her first husband C F Ratcliffe was the nephew of Lord Brotherton, who gave the Brotherton Library to Leeds University, and D U R continued his generosity by donating her Gipsy Collection, one of her many gifts to institutions, art galleries and individual people. She was president of the Yorkshire Dialect Society from 1936 to 1964, and was awarded many local and international honours. She did set great store by her dialect poems, which express deep-felt emotions and a knowledge of dialect words and phrases. But as she was not born to speak dialect, some purists found room for criticism.

In the 1940s after the death of her second husband, she moved to live at Temple Sowerby Manor in the Eden Valley, Cumbria. Here she published a few books and rhyme sheets under the imprint of the Temple Sowerby Press. She gave her house and gardens with an endowment to the National Trust. After her death in 1957, Wilfred Halliday, university lecturer and authority on dialect, sent us his Memoir to D U R, which ended with the words 'Take her for all in all, we shall not look upon her like again'.

In course of time we came to know well Fred Lawson and his wife Muriel, who painted under the name of Muriel Metcalfe, and we became the owners of some of their

Fred Lawson (1888-1968), artist, of Castle Bolton.

beautiful pictures of the dale and of children. But in 1949 it was George Jackson, who lived at Ripon, but who also had a small cottage at Castle Bolton, who used to call. Whilst being his own man, he was part of the coterie of artists and friends who revolved round Fred in those days. The Jackson family business in Ripon (now Phillip Hall) supplied draperies to the dale in the old manner by bringing and delivering goods to individual households. This was not his real interest, for George was a man of many parts, a writer, an artist, and in the 1950s the editor of a magazine the *Wakeman.* In 1957 Marie opened an exhibition of his paintings in Ripon. Striking-looking, he had his portrait painted by Jacob Kramer. He died aged seventy-six in 1974.

Another artist friend was John Greenwood, wood-engraver, who lived at Ilkley. He loved the Dales, and expressed his feelings for them in a book, illustrated with his own engravings, *The Dales are Mine* (1952). These have a distinctive style, epitomised by a lane outlined by walls dipping and rising up to the hills in the far distance. He liked to see what we were doing, and sometimes brought examples of his own work to show us.

Occasionally we had what we called a 'Coleshouse Day'. On 14th June 1949, a diary entry with that heading reads: 'In the morning we spent an hour and a half with the vicar in the church considering what should be done about a new altar table. Then as we were having lunch A J Brown [the writer] and his wife appeared. In the middle of their visit a semi-blind chap called, one of the Yorkshire Bookmen who came last summer ... He did not stay very long. Then we set to work to correct proofs of "Appleby Fair" that had come from *Country Life*, suddenly decided to go to the fair which we knew was being held that day ... when we got there it was pouring down. We motored right through the fair and back'.

A J Brown had been a wing commander in the RAF in the Second World War, and, in 1949, was running a hotel in Goathland together with his wife, which became the subject of a book, *I Bought a Hotel.* They told us that they were thinking of giving it up because of overwork. Born at Bradford, he did return to his post as textile agent. But A J was the ramblers' 'guru', president of the West Riding Ramblers Association for many years, and writing classic books for walkers including *Striding Through Yorkshire*, 1938, *Broad Acres*, 1948, and *Fair North Riding,* dedicated to D U R in 1952. He died in 1969.

In July 1950, Ernest Taylor, a Quaker, and two companions, one a Friend from Indiana, arrived. The American was astonished by our long history — 2,000 years back to the Bronze Age. 'Say that again', he said. We remarked that Mr Taylor looked older, for although we had seen him from time to time, a quarter of a century had passed since he had been responsible for introducing Ella and Marie to Dents.

On 19th September 1950, Geoffrey and Eleanor Winthrop Young called in the morning (and John Greenwood in the afternoon). This was the beginning of a lasting friendship, especially with Len as she preferred to be called, after Geoffrey's death in 1958. They came armed with a small book, entitled *In Praise of Mountains*, an anthology for Friends, compiled by themselves, and with an inscription to the memory of Ella Pontefract.

Geoffrey Winthrop Young was an educationist, and a famous mountaineer — 'one of the greatest England has produced' as the DNB puts it. In the First World War he commanded a Friends Ambulance Unit in Belgium and elsewhere, and as a result of wounds had a leg amputated above the knee, yet remarkably continued to climb. He wrote *On High Hills* (1927), *Mountains with a Difference, Mountain Craft, Collected Poems* (1936) and *The Grace of Forgetting* (1953). Len, too, had links with mountains, for she was the daughter of W C Slingsby, another famous mountaineer, whose family owned a cotton mill at Carleton near Skipton where Len was born, hence her love of Yorkshire and the Dales. They commissioned a watercolour of Ingleborough and a drawing for a small book, *In Praise of Yorkshire*, from Marie. Later in life, Len bought a house between Bainbridge and Askrigg, but her sojourn was cut short by a motor car accident, which stopped her driving, and she moved down south but returned for holidays.

Most, not all, of these friends are dead. Perhaps as new faces take the stage, these notes will remind us of them and their prominence in their day and age. It seems appropriate to end with one of D U R's poems:

Life's like a Fair; a vast of work before
A few hours' fun;
And long ere stars have wested over moor,
Light's out, all's done:
But to each according to our daring
Time gives some Fairing.

A LASTING FRIENDSHIP

Our friendship with Phyllis Bentley began a little before Easter in 1949. On Tuesday 6th April of that year, we had been to a wedding in the village, and as we were recovering over a cup of tea, Marie happened to stand up and saw a figure coming across the green. It was Phyllis Bentley. She was staying at the Rose and Crown Hotel at Bainbridge a mile away. She had decided to call on us without warning on purpose, saying to herself that if we were at home, all well and good, but if we were out, then she was not destined to meet us. Later she also explained that a photograph of Marie somewhat resembled the appearance of her great schoolfriend, Barbara Clark, who had long since left Halifax to go to college, had taken up a career, married and had recently died. Phyllis felt the loss deeply. About the same time Lettice Cooper, the novelist, also a friend, and her sister, Barbara, had left Yorkshire permanently for London, a further blow. Marie's diary records: 'We got on very well'.

The next day we took our visitor's book and our copy of her novel, *Inheritance,* and left them for her to sign at the Rose and Crown. On 8th April we had a visitor who stayed too long, and Joan hung a notice on the front door to say that we were busy and were not to be disturbed. The first person to come to the door and to read the notice was Phyllis, who was returning the books. Fortunately we saw her retreating down the green, and fetched her back. Thus started a rich and lasting friendship.

Phyllis was born at Halifax in the West Riding on 19th November 1894. Her father was involved in the textile industry, and she was the fourth child in the family. The older children were boys, Philip, Norman and Frank, all of whom we often heard about, especially of Frank, her favourite brother. Her mother, who was devoted to her, and to whom Phyllis was devoted, was 'proud, impetuous, loving, ambitious, wilful, vehement, and extremely sensitive', as Phyllis described her in her autobiography *O Dreams O Destinations* (1962). Some of these traits, not always easy ones, were inherited by her daughter. We never knew Mrs Bentley, who died aged ninety, shortly after Phyllis's first visit to us. Her mother made up for occasional scenes by passing on to her daughter her recollections of the textile trade — telling details of inestimable value to a novelist. (Now known as oral tradition, this branch of historical research has been one of the pleasures of our lives.)

Phyllis was of medium height with a pale face and indistinct features. She made a point of dressing well, sometimes appropriately in suits of good West Riding cloth. In 1949 when she, as it were, arrived on our doorstep, she was a little more than a decade older than us, so that we were sometimes made aware of her Victorian background. Also, for a Yorkshire woman we thought her occasionally extravagant, and put this down to the proximity of Halifax to Lancashire, where the inhabitants were reputedly less thrifty than Yorkshire folk. (Such nuances may well seem ridiculous nowadays, when we are all being pressed into the same boring mould.)

In 1949 she was an established novelist on the literary scene, self-assured and not

Phyllis Bentley at her desk in the 1970s.

without self-esteem. *Inheritance*, a bestseller, had made her name seventeen years earlier, and in between she had written five successful novels. She had also experienced four lecture tours in America travelling by train, and had thrived on the warm welcoming hospitality, enhanced by success, and the friendship of her American publishers. She once hinted at a romance over there, and she certainly had a proposal of marriage from someone who she rejected, but who remained a close friend. Once, she told us, she was in her bedroom preparing for a lecture, when she heard through the thin wall a voice reciting a vote of thanks, which, when the lecture ended, turned out to be hers.

Our case was very different. We had yet to re-establish ourselves as a new partnership after the death of Ella Pontefract in 1945. Marie was engaged in writing the tribute to Ella, *Yorkshire Heritage*. This pleased Phyllis, who approved of work going on, but she warned us of the difficulties of making a new start. In 1950 when the book was published she waived her policy of not reviewing friends' books, and wrote a full-page notice of it in *John O' London's Weekly*. The magazine, long since defunct, served a useful purpose, linking authors with the general public. Looking back, we think that it belonged to a nicer world.

In time, a pattern of friendship emerged. We exchanged weekly letters, such as that Phyllis had been to an International PEN conference at Lausanne. Hers were perfectly typed on quarto paper, for she considered good typing to be a necessary skill for an author. (Joan had learnt to type well, but Marie was less proficient.) We also began to exchange monthly visits. Apart from anything else, the journeys across the Pennines were always a pleasure, except in winter when a sudden snowstorm could render the passes treacherous. At Halifax we were usually taken out to lunch at the White Swan Hotel, and often Phyllis drove us to the Rocks, a favourite ravine, or up Calderdale and the Colne Valley to the scenes of her novels. She was never a confident driver, but her car, one of which was called Rooney, because it was maroon-coloured, meant a great deal to her.

In those early days she was living at 8 Heath Villas, supported by a secretary and a daily housekeeper who we came to know well. The house was Victorian, with lofty rooms, a bay window and attics. The many periodicals that Phyllis took were arranged on a table in the bay window, added to later by a maquette of the three Brontës by the sculptor, Jocelyn Horner. On the first floor a large bedroom made a splendid study. There were two tables, many bookcases, a Victorian scrap screen made by her mother, on one wall a map, not of Yorkshire, but of the world, and at either end of the mantelshelf spelter figures of Shakespeare and Milton. In 1950 we attended an At Home in this roomy house. For all its advantages Phyllis did not care for it, and in 1970 she moved to a yeoman-clothier's seventeenth-century house at Warley near Halifax, sharing it with her sister-in-law. This she loved.

At Easter, Phyllis still came to Wensleydale, continuing the 'Thinking Holidays' which she had begun in the 1920s. Sometimes she was at the Rose and Crown, and sometimes she stayed with us. (Friendship had never to interfere with work.) Here we went for walks and often drove to the adjoining quiet countryside of Westmorland to sit eating a picnic near Sunbiggin Tarn, looking at the hordes of nesting gulls and the Howgill hills. One walk was never forgotten. We all agreed to climb Ingleborough, and, on 21st April 1954, cheerfully set off from Clapham to take the longer but less steep route. Towards the end where the gradient increased, Phyllis came to a halt gasping for breath. Very slowly and with many halts we reached the top. 'Never again' we and her family said. We had no idea that she had a weak heart. In 1962 she was in hospital for three weeks with a near-coronary thrombosis, and, brought by her niece, she stayed with us for a further week of convalescence.

At nights during these Easter visits we sat round the fire, talking and playing gramophone records of popular songs. Sometimes we all burst into song. Phyllis never professed to be musical, but she could be delightfully light-hearted and almost childish in the enjoyment of simple pleasures, which struck a chord with us. Once she came to Askrigg by train to spend Christmas with us. We well remember the general air of excitement of meeting her in the dark at the station when other people's relations and friends, coming home for Christmas, were all getting off the train. Such events ceased when the railway closed down in 1954. Once we met at the Spa Hotel at Ripon for Christmas lunch. In order to be private Phyllis commandeered a bedroom where, if anyone had looked in, they would have found three middle-aged to elderly ladies handing each other and opening presents of no particular value, but all prettily wrapped up. Like the Brontës, Phyllis loved little notebooks, and indeed anything to do with the writer's tools.

We revelled in the intelligent conversation, and Phyllis brought news of the Society of Authors, the Royal Literary Society, literature in general, and hers and our work. She was an omnivorous reader, and proudly recollected that in her youth she had catalogued three West Riding libraries, some 80,000 books. She thought that all the books of an author should be read, and after one winter she told us that she had read all the novels of Sir Walter Scott. She believed perhaps controversially that facts known about a writer's life helped towards an understanding of their work. 'Reading, books, literature, they were always my beloved art, my craft, my life from the earliest age I can remember.'

As the years went by, when hers and our new books were published, Phyllis instituted a welcome custom of sending congratulatory telegrams on publication days. Her first book after 1949 was *Quorum*, a collection of short stories which as usual appeared in the familiar yellow jacket favoured by her publishers, Gollancz. Other works followed throughout the 1950s and 1960s, all set in the industrial West Riding, except *Freedom Farewell* (1936) which was inspired by the rise of Hitler and the threat to freedom. Phyllis was a regional novelist of high quality, fiercely attached to her home territory and resisting the call to London.

Perhaps to be fully appreciative of her *oeuvre* the reader has to be West Riding born and preferably connected with the textile industry. The opening paragraph of *Sleep in Peace* (1937) conjures up the West Riding scene in all its drama. (We compare it with the beginning of Hardy's *The Return of the Native*):

> 'It was a wild wet afternoon in the eighteen-nineties. The West Riding of Yorkshire lay harried beneath an Atlantic gale, which, however, it received not prostrate but battling, defiant ... Windows rattled, doors banged ... but in the Hudley engine rooms the great wheels whirred, in the weaving sheds the looms clattered ...'

In her books, real places are given fictitious names, and her characters divide into two groups, the idealists and the materialists, typified by the Bamforths and the Oldroyds in *Inheritance*. Dialect, which appears very seldom, is implied by the occasional use of favourite expressions such as 'Choose how' (anyway). As she herself sometimes said, 'These ingredients were transformed into art in the mental cauldron'.

It has to be remembered that Phyllis was writing before the permissive society took hold. As a leading writer, she was asked to speak for the book at the trial of D H

Lawrence's *Lady Chatterley's Lover*, but declined. *Inheritance* starts with a mild seduction scene, as she herself described it, but anything stronger was out of the question in provincial Yorkshire. She deplored the growing lack of discipline, saying that young people were helped by guidelines. She was an agnostic, deeply concerned for the betterment of mankind, fiercely defensive of the underdog, and in her youth dreaming of making the human mind more capable of perception by culture.

The series of six novels, beginning with *Take Courage* (1940) and continuing, not necessarily written in sequence, with *Manhold* (1941), *Inheritance* (1932), *Carr* (1929), *A Modern Tragedy* (1934) and *Sleep in Peace* (1937), follow the fortunes of the woollen industry and its participants through four centuries, and took her fourteen years to complete. In order to promote foreign trade lost during the 1939-1945 war, Phyllis was asked to write the history of the Yorkshire textile trade by the Huddersfield and District Woollen Export Group. *Colne Valley Cloth* (1947), as it was called, begins 'Cloth has been woven of wool in the Colne Valley for at least six centuries'. Phyllis was rightly proud of this beautifully produced book. At the end of her life the great industry was fading away. She put on record for posterity its grandeur and drama, and the strenuous lives and joys and sorrows of the protagonists.

Speaking on the regional novel in 1925, Phyllis began what amounted to a second career as a lecturer, which led on to the successful American and to English tours. For some reason she never wished us to be present in the audience, so that we heard her speak in public all too seldom. We remember her giving the address at the speech day of our local grammar school in 1961, when she expounded the theme that there were two sorts of people — the administrators and the creators, both equally valuable. Phyllis seems to have combined both. She 'believed with all her heart in the committee as a mode of government'. Her lecture on the Brontës was a tour de force; for she spoke without a note for an hour. As a professional lecturer she once told us that she might produce the occasional note on purpose just to emphasise the expertise of her delivery. Lecturing, which often entailed frequent travel in winter, both earned fees and promoted the sales of her books.

If money was required for something, she would say to herself 'Earn it Phyllis' and earn it she did. Many people benefitted — the family firm, like others sometimes in difficulties, young relations helped with expensive schooling, a fellow novelist down on his luck. The full story of her generosity is so far unknown.

Besides novels she wrote children's books, essays, radio scripts, plays, for many years weekly reviews of novels for the *Yorkshire Post*, and small but valuable books on public speaking, committees, America, and *Some Observations on the Art of Narrative* (1946). The latter is a brilliant exposition of that aspect of the novel. Her books on the Brontës included *The Brontës and Their World, The Young Brontës* illustrated by Marie, and the Heather Edition of the Brontë Works, which she arranged and introduced. They offer some of the best insights into this famous exploited family. Eventually *Inheritance* appeared as a series on television filmed on location, which to Phyllis seemed to crown her career.

Many local societies claimed her attention and support. In her youth she took office as secretary, and later in life as president, often for teens of years. One of her favourites was the Halifax Authors Circle. This group once visited our house. We remember that whilst we all managed to sit on chairs or on the floor in our sitting-room, one member recited her comic party piece 'A Bit of a Hoff', long before Alan Bennett wrote *A Day Out*. Enjoying plays above all other entertainments (and revering Shakespeare), Phyllis supported the Halifax Thespians and the building of a new theatre. She was a member of the 51 Society, and for a time a governor of the BBC. She served on the Council of Leeds University, and on that of the Brontë Society, and was president for eleven years of the Association of Yorkshire Bookmen, then a flourishing society that in time came to an end. She often met scholars from Japan, America, and Brussels at Haworth Parsonage. Later in life she disagreed with the appointment of an unqualified curator at the Parsonage, and so more or less ended contact with the society.

In 1961 we too crossed swords with Phyllis. Our publisher, E F Bozman of J M Dent, suggested that we compile a book on famous men and women born in Yorkshire. Naturally we discussed this with Phyllis, who heartily disapproved. As there seemed no good reason for this hostility, and as we obviously wished to please our publisher, we took up the idea. After reading her profile she commented that 'it was absolutely A1 and admirably written'. But when the book came out, Phyllis disliked her portrait drawn by Marie and wrote angry letters. Marie, who has a gift for obtaining a likeness, had done her best. (Incidentally the bust of her by Jocelyn Horner was destroyed.) This was one of a few disagreements.

Over the years we joined up and went on several holidays together. In 1953 we spent a week at Florence and a week in Venice, with Phyllis, who had been there before, as a splendid guide. We flew to Milan on an Elizabethan airliner, took the train to Florence, and on the way to the hotel by taxi saw Giotto's Tower silhouetted in the moonlight, never to be forgotten. Another holiday was spent in Paris, where again we visited art galleries — the Louvre, and Jeu de Paume, an exhibition of the work of Matisse. These two holidays provided an early opportunity to buy transparencies of famous pictures, so that eventually we built up a comprehensive collection, which led to giving lectures on the history of European art, the study of which became a major hobby, and influenced the start of the Askrigg Art Club.

Other holidays were spent in the Forest of Dean, at Seahouses on the Northumbrian coast, at the Edinburgh Festival, and on the Isle of Man. Lastly in 1967 we all embarked on an ambitious tour to Orkney and the Shetland Islands in our new car, crossing straits from one island to another, and sailing back to Aberdeen. The whole month spent exploring prehistoric and Viking sites, and blessed with good weather, was unforgettable.

For the last ten years of her life Phyllis played a less active role. Other new Yorkshire writers, in whom she took a great interest, appeared. Phyllis moved to a pleasant retirement home at Halifax. In 1949 she had been awarded an Honorary Doctorate from Leeds University, she was made a Fellow of the Royal Literary Society, and in 1970 was given the OBE for services to literature. On 22nd November 1974, Kirklees

The Ring of Brognar, Orkney.

Viking longhouse, Birsay, Orkney.

Joan and Phyllis on the Isle of Man.

Arts Council arranged a literary dinner at Huddersfield to celebrate Phyllis's eightieth birthday, and Marie was asked to propose the toast to her, and Livia Gollancz the toast to literature.

When she died in 1977, a memorial service was held in Halifax Parish Church, attended by relations, friends, colleagues, and admirers. Marie, who found it an ordeal, was asked to give the address, and spoke on behalf of herself and Joan. She described Phyllis, bound up as she was with her native heath, as a 'One Woman Yorkshire Institution'. The tribute was printed in a report of the Royal Literary Society.

YORKSHIRE VILLAGE

As we have seen, we began to explore the possibilities of writing a village history in the autumn of 1950. We found our subject in our own village, Askrigg in Wensleydale, and what is more we found here a village with an extra dimension to its story, for it was formerly a market town. Situated towards the head of Wensleydale, it is at a demarcation point between the wild upper reaches, once the Forest of Wensleydale, and the lower more cultivated dale, in other words the limit of *Domesday Book* in the dale.

There is no doubt that, done properly, writing a village history is a major undertaking. The historian has to try to be an expert on many subjects: climate, geology, church history, farming, aspects of the law, and also a fair knowledge of the history of England, an ever-present background and influence.

Over the years we had built up a library of books essential to our work, such as the classic authorities of the region, amongst which Whitaker, Speight and Clarkson predominate. Also in 1890 Canon Whaley, vicar of Askrigg, had published his history of the village, a good introduction but limited in scope. It has an intriguing list of subscribers, some living as far away as Eastbourne, so that one wonders what their connection was with Askrigg. We also had the general volumes of the *Victoria County History* as well as the two on the North Riding, nine volumes of the *North Riding Quarter Sessions*, some volumes of the Record series of the *Yorkshire Archaeological Society, Records of the Metcalfe Family* (1891), directories of the North Riding, Wright's *English Dialect Dictionary*, and many more general books such as Cox's *The Royal Forests of England* (1950). Other books such as C S Orwin's *The Open Fields* (1938) or Manwood's *Lawes of the Forest* could be borrowed.

When it came to guidance in writing a village history, we bought the *Parish Chest* by W E Tate in its second edition, 1951, and later, in 1967, his *English Village Community*. We corresponded with Mr Tate at Leeds University, and met him once. (W G Hoskins' *Local History in England* was not published until 1959.) We were ahead of our time in researching local history, as will be seen. This had its advantages and disadvantages, as although various offices were not yet started, neither were the ones open as crowded as they are now.

A necessary basic requirement was correct dating. The replacement of the Julian Calendar by the Gregorian in 1752, by which eleven days were lost, had to be mastered, and Gregorian New Style and Julian Old Style dating understood. Also many documents state for instance 'in the second year of King Charles II' instead of giving the actual year. Joan copied out from Sir Maurice Powicke's *Handbook of British Chronologs*, the dates and years of the reigns of the kings of England from Richard I to George V. As one had to know the month when the king came to the throne to fix the date, these lists were invaluable and frequently consulted.

A village history is largely based on documents that broadly speaking are to be found either near at hand in the neighbourhood and at York or Leeds, or far away in London and other places. As winter approached (and as it turned out a bad one), we started on documents near at hand. Obtaining permission from the vicar, we borrowed many papers from the Armada Chest in the church. At that date all the muniments, including the parish registers, were stored there, and have since been taken to the County Record Office. We had no need to borrow the registers as there were transcripts available made by our old friend, J J G Lodge, who had found Ella Pontefract and Marie their cottage. For the local historian, parish registers are without price, and we kept the transcripts by us almost all the time we were engaged on the book.

One day returning from the church, we remembered that one of the houses in the village street was being sold, and so we stopped off to attend the sale. Bidding was slow, and the sand glass used to mark the end was run out twice to reach the sum of £770. Today such a house would rather make £70,000.

In November, again with permission, this time from the headmaster of Yorebridge Grammar School, we spent Saturdays in his study taking notes from the school archives. These, together with information from other sources, built up the often contentious story of the school. Here, too, was a cupboard housing the McFie collection of books bought by public subscription for local use when R A Scott McFie died in 1935. A recluse, living at Lunds in upper Wensleydale, he hailed from Liverpool.

A year or two before his death Ella Pontefract and Marie had met him and worked at Lunds on his collections of local history. Amongst these were several original Askrigg township books, such as the leather-bound *Book of the Four Men*, the four men being the precursors of the parish council. McFie had found several of these treasures in an antiquarian bookshop in Liverpool, and we were able to borrow them. Anything that could be studied at home saved precious time. By November we were ready to send a synopsis to Bozzie, and whilst his response was favourable, he asked for clarification and to see three chapters.

1951 was a busy year. *The Old Hand-Knitters* had yet to be published in June, and when it came out,we spent a few days visiting old friends who had helped in order to present them with copies. One was Marmaduke Clarkson, the vet for upper Swaledale and his sister at Satron, who had lent us the Clarkson ledger kept by his fore-elders, who were millers at Satron mill, now gone, except for foundations. They were charming reminders of old Swaledale. There followed the York Festival and the Grandmothers Treasures exhibition, which all took up time. We also attended with our friend, Phyllis Bentley, one of the first performances of the York Mystery Plays, staged sparingly, and a moving memorable experience. As well this was the year of the Festival of Britain, celebrated in London with ambitious displays intended to boost the morale of the nation after the war. We managed to visit it in conjunction with taking Joan's mother back to Hampshire after a holiday with us. Marie describes the Festival, which we enjoyed, as 'a glorified educational Butlin's'.

However, at the beginning of this year, 1951, we started work in earnest, Joan tackling the Quarter Sessions records, and towards the end of the month we visited the library of the Yorkshire Archaeological Society, then at 10 Park Place, Leeds. Here Amy Foster, the librarian, partly because there were so few people there, gave us special attention. She and Marie confessed that they had Matriculation Latin, but whereas Miss Foster was fluent, Marie had forgotten most of hers — a great pity. There was obviously so much work to be done there, that in early February we stayed with Marie's brother and his wife for a working week, and went through the 200 volumes of the State Papers, the journals of the society, and many deeds. We read in the journals of 'the road that leads to the church at Askrigg' in 1218, the first direct reference to a church here. Hours of apparently useless work were rewarded by such discoveries.

Having obtained readers' tickets for the Public Record Office in Chancery Lane, London, we arrived there on 25th April. We made our way to the Search Room, a small, round, warren-like room with lighting high up in the central roof, and walls lined with catalogues headed at the top of each section 'Exchequer', 'Augmentation Office' etc. We used references from the Calendars of State Papers seen at Leeds and from the Victoria County History, and although one of the attendants was helpful, it was a daunting task finding details about one small village in all the welter of documents relating to the whole of England. The first lot brought to us was an enormous bundle of blackened parchments that stretched one way and unrolled down another. Somehow or other Marie had learnt by experience to read Elizabethan and seventeenth century court hand, or we should have been undone.

In the end, after a week we had to leave with work outstanding, and we arranged for an agent, Miss Drucker, to continue research for us. At the end of the year in late December, we again visited London (and Dents), and spent two days in the Public Record Office, one day in the South Room looking at Chancery Proceedings. The assistant remembered us and was particularly helpful. Miss Drucker had retired, and a new agent, Miss N McNeil O'Farrell, who was splendid and knew the kind of material we wanted, took on our work.

The search in London, revealing new aspects of the village history never even hinted at before, was invaluable. We learnt of the market charter, granted in 1587 to Peter Thornton who was later indicted for felony, of later disputes over the market tolls, and of the petition of the inhabitants of Hawes for a market and fairs in 1699, of the Book of Horses and Mares taken off Flodden Field, 1513, in which a witness told of how he had seen the last abbot of Jervaulx and his monks come riding up Wensleydale to view their property on Abbotside. Another document of 1609 actually mentioned 'ranes', the strips in the open fields of the village. In Elizabethan times the corn mill was often in disrepair; an agreement to keep a parish bull caused a law suit; and details of the Yorkshire Plot, a Nonconformist reaction to various restrictive acts, enlarged on what we had found in Leeds.

After staying in London, where we had driven by car for the Festival of Britain, we motored to Cambridge to visit Trinity College, which after the Dissolution owned the tithes of the parish of Aysgarth, which included the parish of Askrigg, until they were commuted in the 1840s. We had obtained permission from the senior bursar to spend two or three days there, and we were installed in an alcove in the famous library with a large tin box labelled 'Aysgarth', filled with bundles of documents. On the second day the librarian allowed us to stay locked in after the closing time of 4 pm for another three hours, as he had extra work to do elsewhere. We complained that the seats, elegant wooden flat-topped benches, were hard, and were told that they were part of the original design by Sir Christopher Wren. We had pointed out to us the rooms of the Master of Trinity, G M Trevelyan. This visit, too, resulted in obtaining fascinating new material, for instance that tithe barns had once existed at Thoralby,

The Wren Library, Trinity College, Cambridge.

West Burton and Newbiggin, and that the college had often been besieged by letters asking for increases in stipends. Trinity still has the gift of the advowson to nominate the vicar of Aysgarth. Somehow it is an extraordinary connection with that wonderful college. We returned by Ely in order to see the cathedral, and arrived home after clocking in 711 miles.

Meanwhile, in between these excursions there was work to be done at home. Towards the end of June we first became acquainted with C Croft Andrew, who some eighteen months previously had been appointed county archivist for the newly-founded County Record Office at Northallerton. For us this was timely. At first, inundated with pioneer work, he was lukewarm, casting doubt on the viability of a village history, but soon taking a personal interest and offering every facility in his then cramped quarters. We shall not forget when he once wrote that he had found something he thought would interest us. It was the incomplete but marvellous diary of Alexander Fothergill, long thought to be lost. Alexander, brother of Dr John Fothergill, a famous Quaker physician and founder of Ackworth School near Pontefract, lived at Carr End, near Semerwater, and was surveyor of the Richmond to Lancaster turnpike road begun in 1751. We were allowed to borrow this, and Joan typed it all out. Much later, when the diary and its ancillary papers were published in a bulletin of the Record Office, this came in useful. Croft Andrew and his assistant, Mrs A Hill, proved to be staunch supporters of our project. In July we paid two visits to the Ripon Diocesan Registry in Leeds, where the registrar, G Errington Wilson, allowed us to see bishops' visitations, terriers and so on, plus the tithe award and accompanying map giving all the field names. We had to go out and buy large sheets of tracing paper in order to copy the map.

Errington Wilson also arranged for us to see the papers of the Archdeaconry of Richmond Consistory Court, then in the Church Institute in Leeds. He warned us that the documents were 'in a very dusty and dirty condition, and contained in sacks and unindexed ... for the time being anyone who inspects them is undertaking a rather unpleasant job'. We did go there towards the end of September, and were locked in a sort of cage. As we picked out the papers from the sacks, dust flew, and some disintegrated from age and damp. Later we felt slightly off-colour. Here wills were proved, recusants listed and visitations recorded. We also learnt that the court formerly acted as guardians of morals, allocating demeaning punishments, such as standing in church draped in a white sheet for moral lapses. One choice extract told us that Christopher Alderson, a dyer, was fined £4 for 'hanging out his stockings to dry upon Sondayes'. Dyeing was of course connected with the knitting industry. These papers were moved to the Central Library, Leeds, in 1952, and are now lodged at the Leeds Archives Department in Chapeltown Road, Leeds.

Meanwhile, fieldwork waited to be tackled. In March we walked the East and West Fields and plotted the ridges of the strips, which were plain to see, on a large-scale map. We submitted the map to Professor Maurice Beresford, who we happened to be seeing at the time. The map revealed that Askrigg was a nucleated village, formerly with open fields cultivated in strips where corn was grown. Sometimes, especially in the East Field, a feeling of great age enveloped us, as the now-grassy fields surged up to the outskirts of the village.

One day in August we planned to view the scene at dawn from Ellerkin, the limestone scar to the north of the village. Our first attempt ended in failure, as although we rose at 4am, mists obscured the valley. Our second succeeded, and proved to be an exhilarating experience, fully recorded in *Yorkshire Village*. A second different sortie came off when we sat in the car in the market place, and plotted the start of a day in village life. This caused a mild stir, and friends asked what we were doing.

In time the richness of surviving church records became apparent, all relevant to a village history, but threatening to overwhelm. There was still the York Diocesan Registry, in the charge of Dr J S Purvis. On our first visit the records were housed in a chamber in a corner of the Minster buildings near the south door, as far as we remember a long, cave-like place with shelves filled with bundles of documents. Dickens, in *Household Words* (1850), describes a visit to this room, its cramped, smoky quarters, and unhelpful clerks. Cramped it certainly was, but a far from unhelpful custodian.

Dr Purvis edited the York Mystery Plays as performed at the York Festival, and compiled *Tudor Parish Documents in the Diocese of York*. He and his sister invited us to lunch, and in return they came to Askrigg. We admired and respected his scholarship as we had done that of Croft Andrew. An important document found for us was a dispute concerning Yorebridge Grammar School occurring only twenty years after its foundation. When they were in Latin, he translated other documents. We learnt of 'monuments of superstition', that is rood lofts and figures, abhorred at the Reformation, whose destruction was a permanent loss to posterity. At the courts of the Archdeaconry of Richmond, punishments for misdemeanours were meted out; one man, John Nicholson of Carperby, was fined for saying 'The preaching of the Gospel is but bibble babble. I had rather hear a Cuckowe sing.'

There was still much to do in York. The second time we visited the diocesan registry, it had moved to new premises, the Borthwick Institute, then newly opened, but still with Dr Purvis in charge. On the other hand the York Probate Registry, which held wills and inventories from Tudor times, was a public office for registering deaths, so that researchers had to take turns with bereaved people. Into the bargain the registrar was notoriously difficult, and once in front of us reduced a researcher to tears. One afternoon, far too early, he told us that we could see no more wills. Now these are lodged at the Borthwick Institute.

There remained the York Minster Library, then not catalogued but with the Horsfall Turner collection, in which we found poor copies of Askrigg manor court rolls (better than nothing) and the will of the Rev John Dupont of Aysgarth, which came in for a profile of Dupont in our book *A Dales Heritage*. At the Central Library, York, we asked our good friends there for all the copies of the *York Courant* and *York Chronicle*, then in a limited way our local papers. Large bound volumes had to be brought up on a lift. Time again was our enemy.

In early September we began to write the first chapter. A village history resembles a biography, not of a person but of a place. Although we had not 'birthright

Askrigg from Coleshouse garden.

Askrigg main street in the winter of 1979.

Askrigg from Abbey Heads, with Yorebridge Grammar School and Askrigg Station as it was.

membership' as Quakers say, of the village community, we, like a biographer, had amassed a great deal of knowledge about it, and were engrossed in our subject. It so happened that during the writing of our history two public events occurred — the election of district and parish councillors, and the proclamation of the accession to the throne of Queen Elizabeth II on the death of George VI. All the accumulation of fieldwork, knowledge of the past and current events coalesced into our story.

In late November we posted the first two chapters to Dents and waited anxiously. Bozzie wrote, 'I am delighted to be able to say that I am most favourably impressed by your specimen chapters, and I believe you have the making of a very successful book'. Dick, too,was asked to read the first chapter, and wrote: 'I thoroughly enjoyed a charming piece of prose. It is good'. It was not known then that Joan wrote poetry, and contributed a lyrical slant to the writing. On 12th January 1952 we signed a contract with Dents to publish the book, to be completed by 1st November 1952. It is worth recording the continual escalation of the costs of book production. Dents explained that paper was nearly six times as much as it used to be twenty years ago, and printing and binding three times as much. Yet published prices had only doubled.

Again, in early January 1952 we began work in earnest. There was the council offices at Hawes for rate books, valuations, and the award for the enclosure of the Commons in 1819. A thick file of letters accumulated; from the Bodleian Library who sent a photocopy of part of the Gough map; the British Museum (which we had visited), who sent particulars of their copies of the *Wensleydale Advertiser* published in the 1840s; the College of Arms in London, who tried but failed to find the coats of arms of two Askrigg families, one the Pratts; the Newby Hall estate linked with Nappa Hall and the Metcalfes; British Rail at York, where we met an old railwayman who deplored nationalisation and said that all personal touch had gone. W V Wade of Leeds University wrote us a short note on the Roman fort at Bainbridge, and others helped with lists of birds and flowers.

Lastly came recollections of the immediate past, which revealed poverty, itinerants passing through, and characters who took little regard for the opinions of others. When she was visiting her mother in Hampshire, Joan tracked down an exciseman and his wife at Milford-on-Sea, who had lived at Askrigg and witnessed the Askrigg flood in 1908, and had first-rate recollections of it. One fine sunny day we were pressed to visit a house in the main street, and slightly resented having to spend time indoors. We found the fire lit in the parlour, and our old friend, who had recently retired with her husband from a lonely farm, settled down, sitting on the floor at our feet to talk. She spoke of many things, of seeing a figure dressed in Cavalier clothes looking out of a window in the Old Hall, and of her father who remembered hearing the horn of the mail coach as it passed up dale on the road on the other side of the valley. This would be in the 1840s.

At the end of our research we had fifteen loose-leaf notebooks crammed with material, each notebook devoted to one subject such as 'Early References'. We now have them filed under their separate headings, and still sometimes refer to them in 1995.

We posted the manuscript to Dents in February 1953, three months late according to the date in our contract. Dick Chapman, who had read the completed work, wrote, 'Never again must you work against time like this'. Production went ahead. Photographs once envisaged were dropped, and maps, plans, graphs and pen-and-ink drawings agreed on. For the wrapper and frontispiece we submitted a watercolour of a view from Askrigg Town Head in winter under snow, but this was eventually rejected in favour of a summer scene of the same view. In June 1953 we visited London, and were taken out to lunch to Rules by Martin Dent, head of production, and one night we had dinner at the Ivy with Marie's niece who was working in London. Then, in September we spent a fortnight in Italy at Florence and Venice with our friend Phyllis Bentley.

Yorkshire Village was published at 18s on 12th November 1953, and was well reviewed in both local and national papers. Professor Beresford wrote approvingly in the *Economic History Review*, but wished that we had added footnotes to the text. Unwilling to put off the general reader, we had only listed our sources in an appendix, and now regret the decision. A J Brown said, in the *Yorkshire Observer,* 'to write a carefully documented history of a Dales village is a formidable task calling for imagination, industry, and courage of the highest order.' The review in the *Times Literary Supplement* ended with: 'The authors living a Dales life have a deep understanding of the Dales people whose story deserves to be — and is — well told.' The bookshops, W H Smith at Harrogate and Walkers of Leeds, put on special displays and invited us to signing sessions.

Following publication, letters poured in. Reading them now is both a sad, for so many people have gone, and a heart-warming experience. Friends at record offices thanked us for copies sent in return for their help. Two who had compiled village histories, H Bradfer-Lawrence and the Rev H H V de Candole, Suffragan Bishop of Knaresborough, gave us their books. The bishop sent messages of congratulation, and he and his wife came to tea. Kit Calvert wrote that 'he had read it, at leisure, and found it the best book I have read for years'. Laurie Town, Dick's friend, offered to bind us a copy in leather. Dents were pleased.

On 22nd January 1954 we gave a lecture to a crowded audience of the Wensleydale Society. Dick Chapman took the chair. Afterwards many people came and congratulated us, and the president suggested that we have the lecture printed. A stranger needlessly tried to carp by remarking on very minor points. When we gave the same lecture to the Yorkshire Archaeological Society in Leeds, Dr Purvis, then the president, was suitably at the meeting. Chairs ran out, and some of the audience had to sit on the floor. At Askrigg on 17th February we gave the same lecture to another full meeting of the Women's Institute, including several men. The secretary, giving the vote of thanks, said that they were losing much (the railway had recently finished), but they would always have THE BOOK. Our local newsagent sold over 100 copies. The book was translated into braille. It was reprinted in 1979, and brought out as a paperback in 1989 by Smith Settle, so that it is still in print.

THE YORKSHIRE DALES

Early in January 1954 we began to seek inspiration for the subject of a new book. At the time the National Parks, including the Yorkshire Dales, were being set up, and were in the news. To proceed from a village history to the story of the Dales in general seemed a logical step. So on 6th January we wrote to Bozzie at Dents informing him of a proposed book on the Dales and mentioning the National Parks. At first he thought that others might rush in on the new subject, but later wrote that we must not hurry because of 'the high quality, originality and authenticity on which your reputation has been built'. On 19th January we sent him a synopsis defining our area as that of the National Park, which included the main dales but excluded Nidderdale and Teesdale. Whether to leave out these two dales or not became a sticking point. To resolve it, we went to London at the end of January, and spent an hour and a half discussing the proposed book at Dents. Although the matter was left unresolved, on 3rd February we were offered a contract for a book of 90,000 words, plus drawings, maps, plans, a colour jacket and appendices, with a completion date of 31st December 1955. The decision on the actual area drifted on. Publishers always want as large an area as possible for topographical books. But in the end, in order to give maximum wordage to the main dales and the side valleys, we stuck to the National Park, a compact region of 680 acres.

It is surprising how much social life we managed to fit in during these two years. Both our mothers came to stay at different times in 1954, and we were also giving the lectures on 'Writing a Village History'. Later in the year, besides others, we gave three lectures on consecutive days to members of the Association of Yorkshire Bookmen at Batley, Cleckheaton and Huddersfield. On another occasion in July 1955, a party of eighty-nine members of the York Georgian Society came to view mansions in Wensleydale, and took in our cottage on their tour.

Towards the end of the year we appeared on television for the first time in a women's programme called *Leisure and Pleasure* organised by Olive Shapley, a friend of Joan's and a well-known broadcaster. For this we drove to Manchester and stayed two nights at the Midland Hotel, rehearsing the first afternoon at Belle Vue, again on the following morning, and finally going on the air at 4.15pm. Three or four others took part. A delightful cosmetic expert dried up, and Olive had to rush to the rescue. We answered questions reasonably well, and some of our books and pictures illustrated the programme. Another participant was Violet Carson, who later became famous as Ena Sharples in *Coronation Street.* An old trooper, she had been a professional pianist playing at cinemas. She kindly said that we had done well. Marie wrote in her diary that when all was over, 'Relief was universal'. We had dinner with Olive and her husband in their own home, and returned to Wensleydale the next day.

For some reason we stopped off at Leeds City Station, and for the first time experienced the spurious fame that an appearance on TV offers. An assistant in the

Crummackdale.

refreshment rooms said 'I saw you on television last night', and a man passing by asked 'Have you room for me in your cottage?'. When we reached Wensleydale, snow had fallen heavily, and we slid, skidded and scraped home. On another occasion we appeared on Yorkshire Television's programme *Clegg's People* with Arthur Scargill, then at the height of his popularity. Coalmines were not mentioned; for he and his wife had brought along their huge pedigree Airedale dogs. From time to time an invitation to take part in TV programmes came along. At least one was there to speak for oneself. Sometimes profiles in newspapers seem to have invented part of the article.

Whilst in London at the end of January, we had again visited the Public Record Office, and had met Miss N McNeill O'Farrell, who introduced us to Miss Coates and her assistants from the National Register of Archives. They showed us their system and indices. When next in London in June, we went to their offices, for here were kept slips for the Victoria County History of the West Riding, which had been started but never completed. Parts of the Dales were of course in the West Riding. Here we made the surprising discovery of at least ten famous men who had been born in and around Sedbergh. One was a Marian martyr, others schoolmasters, clerics, and physicians amongst the last were John Dawson, surgeon and mathematician (1734-1820), Anthony Fothergill (1732?-1813), John Haygarth, infectious diseases

(1740-1827), and Robert Willan, dermatologist (1751-1812). In more recent years, medical historians have written up some of these.

Meanwhile, we had begun work, with Joan making a synopsis of each chapter, which covered the main dales from Wharfedale to Swaledale and Arkengarthdale. A fair amount of research was a repetition of that for *Yorkshire Village*, except of course our horizon was more extensive. In late February 1954, for instance, we stayed with Marie's brother and his wife in Leeds to spend a week at the library of the Yorkshire Archaeological Society. In mid-March we were at County Hall and at York Minster libraries and examining the Archdeaconry of Richmond Consistory Court papers. This time the Archdeaconry papers had been rescued from the sacks, and were to be seen at Leeds Public Library, eventually as we have said to be lodged at the Leeds Archives Department, Sheepscar.

True to form in making use of relatives, we stayed from 30th March to 3rd April with Joan's cousin, Christabel Ingilby, at her charming cottage at Austwick. As her family had formerly lived at Lawkland Hall, and as she was born at Austwick, she herself gave us inimitable insights into the district. This limestone country was new to us. Exploring it, we found Crummackdale, the Norber boulders, hidden hamlets, and towering above all, Ingleborough, a favourite and majestic hill. Christabel introduced us to Christopher Cheetham, a dedicated naturalist, who took us on a walk on Oxenber in search of grasses and flowers; and also at the hamlet of Wharfe she introduced us to an elderly couple who had lived for forty years at Cosh at the head of Littondale, and for twenty years had farmed at Crummackdale. Having lived far from neighbours for so long, they seemed to us 'untarnished from the world'. Christabel had donated Elizabethan court rolls from the manor of Lawkland to the Yorkshire Archaeological Society, and following these up we learnt of the burden imposed on tenants who had to grind their corn at the local mill, repair it, thatch the kiln, and take on the job of corn drier. The former importance of corn mills in the lives of villagers is forgotten.

From Austwick we visited Tot Lord and his museum at Town Head, Settle. It was one of several visits, and once or twice Tot called to see us at Askrigg. Here we saw artefacts from the Victoria and other caves near Settle, evidence of early settlement from Mesolithic times onwards. Naturally this was to make the beginning of our story of the Dales. A born collector, with an eye for finding hidden objects, Tot had buckets full of flints, and once told us that while visiting Star Carr, a famous site near the Yorkshire coast, after the archaeologists had finished and gone, he had picked out several Mesolithic objects. The museum also housed important documents and old photographs, some of which we were lent to study at home. Amongst these were copies of the *Settle Chronicle* dating from 1854 and, like the *Wensleydale Advertiser* of the 1840s, giving glimpses of the ways of life of those times. There were advertisements for tar and butter used in sheep salving, news of servants changing places at Whitsuntide, several fairs in full swing, tallow chandlers, dyeworks, a ropewalk, and a tilery for sale.

Reports in the paper of the prizewinners at the North Ribblesdale Agricultural

Association Exhibition gave us a breakthrough in information on the baking of oatcake such as the researcher dreams of. We knew that during its long career the method of baking oatcake had changed. In September 1854, a premium of £1 was offered for 'a Basket of Oatcake containing Six Cakes'. A year later the premium offered was for oatcake 'made on the new system'. Formerly the oatmeal batter was thrown on to the bakestone, described as 'an art in itself', but now in the 'new style' it was poured on and a wooden implement trailed across it to make the typical oval shape. Thus we learnt of the date of the changeover in baking oatcake. This seems a small matter, but it is the stuff that research is made of.

On Sunday 11th April we set off for Chatsworth House in Derbyshire, in order to consult the archives relating to the Bolton Abbey estates at Skipton, Wharfedale and elsewhere. The owners, the Dukes of Devonshire, had inherited these by marriage through the Earl of Burlington, so that we expected eighteenth century papers to predominate, but found many of an earlier date. The archivist, T S Wragg, had booked rooms for us at the Peacock at Baslow. The first night, a friend of Marie's came from Chesterfield to have dinner with us. Her father, secretary of Sheepbridge Iron and Coal Company, had arranged the visit of Ella Pontefract and Marie to Maltby Main Colliery in 1939, recorded in *Yorkshire Tour.*

Next day we arrived at Chatsworth House, and took ten minutes to reach the library where we were to work. As the landowners had been absentee landlords, correspondence with agents prevailed. Lead-mines at Cockbarr on Grassington Moor, Gavel mines and Birks Smelt Mill at Buckden, and Threshfield Colliery were let. Some lead from Cockbarr went to Skipton Castle and some for shot. In 1742 a wooden bridge was built at Hubberholme, and several new barns, often replacing old ones, were built round Bolton. This and other information relating to barns and the deer we found invaluable much later for *Dales Memories.* A deer keeper and a wood ruff were appointed, and distraints made on people who could not pay their rents. One of these at Storiths had an ox yoke and bows. Mr Wragg was so helpful and the documents so fascinating that regrettably we had no time to look round the house or the garden.

In May almost daily sorties were made, to talk to Tom Gill at Reeth, a splendid informant, to Bradford to the public library and Cartwright Hall to consult the notes left by Harry Speight, of no use to us, and to Malhamdale, Ribblesdale and Giggleswick. At the end of the month Mr and Mrs H L Bradfer-Lawrence invited us to lunch to see the estate papers of the Listers, Lord Ribblesdale of Gisburn. We spent the afternoon in their muniment room examining these. In 1785, Lord Ribblesdale acquired the northern half of Malhamdale, so we read that Malham Tarn House had been enlarged, trees planted and the level of the lake raised, and that calamine, zinc, lead and copper were mined during Malhamdale's brief industrial history. The calamine was sold to the Cheadle Brass Company for making brass, and sometimes they complained that the calcination had been badly done. In one mine stalactites and stalagmites were broken off, and sold in Bond Street, London, as natural curiosities. Lists of the farms on Malham Moor gave acreages, and details such as Water Houses had

Deepdale.

been called the Lodge for the Keeper of the Fishery and for the Foresters of the Forest of Knoupe. These archives are now at the library of the Yorkshire Archaeological Society.

Another visit was to Draycott Hall at Fremington in Swaledale, which came about because Joan knew the then owner, Mrs M Radcliffe, a direct descendant of the Denys family, notable for their development of the mines in their heyday. It was fascinating to see hanging on the walls portraits of Lord Pomfret, owner of the mineral rights in the eighteenth century, and of Peter Denys who married his daughter, and to be shown the agent's office containing tables laden with lead-mining papers. Later we took notes from these papers, but full use was made of them by Bernard Jennings for an MA thesis on lead-mining. They are now lodged at the County Record Office. On the lawn in front of the house stood a statue of a bearded man seated on pigs of lead, which personified the planet Saturn, which to chemists typified lead. This is no longer there.

Lead-mining had never been one of our major interests, partly because other people were specialists, and partly because, although the human interest appealed to us strongly, mining seemed very technical. When the local historian E R Fawcett of Muker died, his widow offered us his collection of manuscripts and original documents, which included the Parke Diary, the Wadeson letter book, and so on, and we contributed to lead-mining history by writing up some of these later in *A Dales Heritage.* All these documents too are now at the County Record Office.

In between there were walks. Whilst staying with Christabel Ingilby in the spring, we had climbed Penyghent, and had seen purple saxifrage in flower. In April we went

Gunnerside.

up Ingleborough with Phyllis Bentley, an experience already related earlier in this book. In August we went on several walks with Dick Chapman, to Victoria Cave, on the old road up Whernside in Dentdale, another to Tan Hill to explore the remains of coalmines, and on a lovely day in a period of poor weather we walked up Crummackdale.

On 8th May 1954 we returned blacksmiths' ledgers lent to us by William Calvert of Gunnerside. The Calverts were well-known to us, for one of the fore-elders, William, had settled at Askrigg as blacksmith and innkeeper, a usual combination of occupations, and although he had died in 1926, his daughter Margaret Anne and other relations lived on. We well remember one of them coming to tell us that we must talk to Miss Calvert, and we hastened to do so, and heard the story of her walk at the age of eight in the 1870s from Burnley, where William, her father, had lived for a time, to Gunnerside for the Methodist Midsummer Festival, and how she had run about picking up goose feathers, and had sat on the pastures which were 'clad with people'. At Gunnerside in 1954 the smithy still contained lead-mining relics. Memories of the demise of the mines lingered on.

That day in May, after delivering the ledgers, we set off up Gunnerside Gill. If anywhere spells lead-mining it is surely Gunnerside and Gunnerside Gill. Perhaps Beldi Hill and Swinnergill near Keld run them a close second. The walk, described in *The Yorkshire Dales*, culminates in Blakethwaite Smelt mill, standing up on a spit of land with its surface chimney running up a scar. Joan's notes read: 'It is like looking at the remains of an old abbey, the romantic situation, the desolation, the feeling of loneliness, the idea that life has gone from the place overcomes one and fills one with awe'.

Work continued. On 23rd October 1954 the chapters on Wharfedale were completed. (A few days later, staying at Leeds with Marie's brother, whilst giving the Bookmen Lectures, four of us had lunch at Marshalls, then a first-class department store, at a cost of £1 15s.) The weather in October hampered our progress. On four days running in November we visited Dentdale, the 'terrestrial paradise' of Adam Sedgwick, and a favourite and familiar dale since we wrote *The Old Hand-Knitters of the Dales*. It appears to have caught the fancy of our agent at the Public Record Office, because we have files of transcripts from chancery proceedings, ministers' accounts and Exchequer special commissions, much of it concerned with quarrels over the ownership of property, some on the five corn mills of Dent, which we used to good purpose in *Dales Memories*.

At Dent Station the young station master told us that he had gone there because of Ella Pontefract's and Marie's books, and added that the local people were a very closed community. At Deepdale Head we walked to the farm from the road, and knocked at the door. A woman's voice asked who we were and what did we want? After we explained, she opened the door, saying 'I suppose you're honest, decent folk'. She spoke of the many little farms in Deepdale, some in ruin, some empty. This was a recurrent theme, for these 'lile spots' had grown from assarts in the forest, many with as little as six acres and often occupied by large families. They were ill-equipped to withstand the harsh realities of the Industrial Revolution. In the last century, building walls for the enclosures of the commons, building the Settle-Carlisle line, the hand-knitting industry even in its decline, the Stone House marble works and the many craftsmen still flourishing had kept the dale alive.

We met men and women with vivid recollections of the old Dent. There was Mr Burton, born in 1856 at Cowgill, Dent, who spoke of the knitting and of a horse fair at Kirk Bridge, Dent Town, and George Fothergill who was born at Myers Garth, Deepdale, in 1877. They had two fields, two cows and sold milk, 'You could live on 2s 6d a week and farm produce'. He was a builder and mason. Betsy Parrington, born in 1863, recollected the Tuesday market when the bellman, Laurence Thistlethwaite, cried 'Draw up', Draw up', and of Dent Fair at Whitsuntide when stalls lined the streets and 'you could walk on people's heads', when shooting galleries, roundabouts, swing boats and striking machines arrived. 'It was a Dent i' them days'. 'Nobody 'at ever came to Dent mended it' said another.

By chance we found and became friends with Jim Capstick and his sister, who lived at Tofts under Combe Scar. On our first visit Jim talked for two and a half hours on the quarrels before the enclosures, of hirings, of people knitting under their plaids, of tumble-cars in which the wheel and axle were one piece, of old men sitting in huts to shoot ravens, of washing and salving sheep, when they would be wet through all day. 'No wonder that old men were walking on sticks'. We also met the Ellisons at Greenwell, a family that had moved to Liverpool to a milk house, but on account of their health had returned. Forty years on our friends, George and Mary Ellison, now in their eighties, keep up by telephone, and we visit them annually.

Our last expedition in 1954 was to Littondale, and on 20th November, by working until 9.30.pm, we finished the chapter on Dent. Bad weather followed, with snow falling in January, and then in earnest in February with snow stowering, cars over-blown, and Semerwater frozen over. But the dark days were good for working. Phyllis Bentley was badly bitten by a dog at a moorland farm, and a week or two later fell and broke her wrist and could not write. A reporter from the *Northern Echo* came and wrote a 'Plain good account of us'. The snow slowly wasted away.

In early March, Marie's friend from childhood, Eva Johnson, came to stay for a rest following the death of her father. Many years later when she died, she astounded everyone by leaving £2,000,000, half donated to the National Trust and half to animal charities. Towards the end of April, Professor Maurice Beresford brought a party of students from Leeds University to look at the medieval field system, and they picniced on the flags in front of the cottage.

There was still some fieldwork and drawings to be made. Marie accomplished these in the brilliant hot summer of 1955. But the year was blighted by the illness and death of Marie's brother, Allan, the head of the family and of the family firm. We were torn between work and sorrow. However, chapters were written, some for instance, Swaledale, turning out longer than we expected and being divided into three sections. Failing to finish by 31st December 1955, the date for completion on our contract, we spent Christmas at Scarborough. Returning home, we worked very hard, and posted off the manuscript at the end of the January. Maps and plans were still outstanding. On receipt of the manuscript Bozzie wrote: 'You have produced a very fine and comprehensive book. I see that the information given is chiefly historical and topographical with occasional lively references to present-day social conditions and ways of life. It is a good solid and conscientious piece of work'.

The appendices included plans and a brief history of castles and abbeys, a gazetteer of dales churches, population figures from 1801 to 1951, regional recipes, a dialect glossary and a bibliography. For the plans we had to obtain permission from the relevant offices to reproduce them. The recipes came from Arkengarthdale, given to us by Mrs W H Hutchinson, whose husband was the gamekeeper there, and whose daughter Elinor was the wife of one of our friends at Keld. She also gave us a wooden stamp with a heart motif for pressing on funeral cakes, a treasure preserved in the Dales Countryside Museum.

As the routine of production of the book proceeded, we enjoyed the highlight of the late summer of 1956, a trip to Paris with Phyllis Bentley. We saw the famous treasures of the Louvre, and were struck by the number of copyists, one woman bravely copying the *Mona Lisa* amidst a large crowd. We saw the sights of Paris, some of which Marie made crayon drawings. We heard *Boris Godounov* at the opera, and visited the Sorbonne, which pleased Phyllis. Towards the end of October we were in London, and were bowled over by the Braque exhibition at the Tate Gallery.

Joan and Phyllis at the top of the Eiffel Tower.

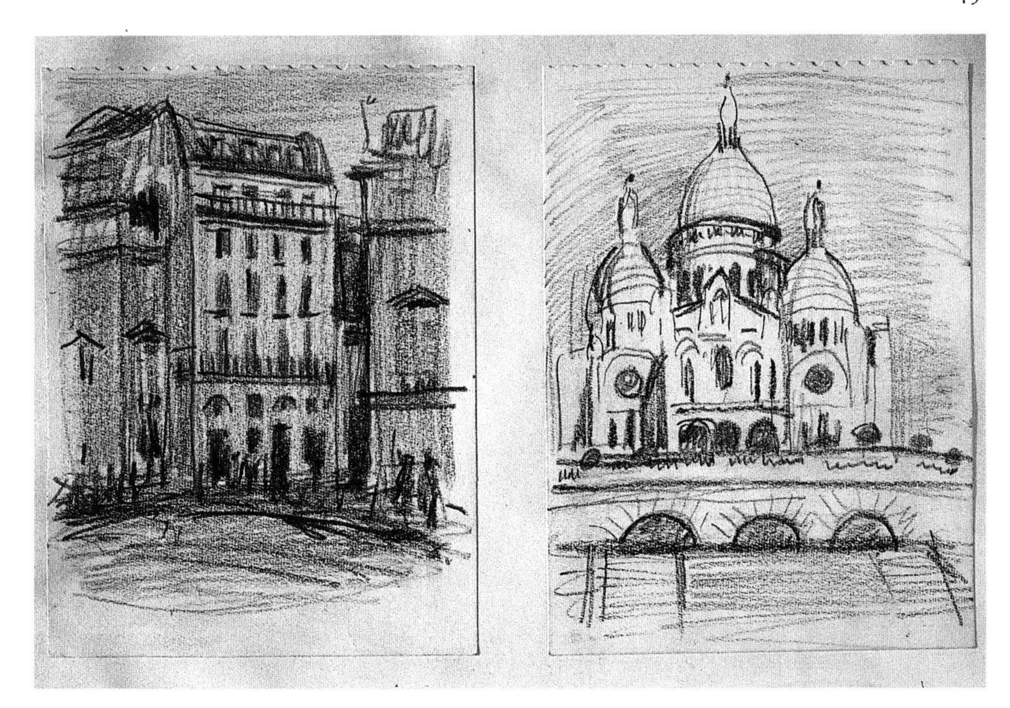

Four crayon drawings of Paris by Marie.

The Yorkshire Dales was published on 18th October, and was favourably received. We only know this from letters, as somehow the reviews from the *Observer, The Sunday Times,* the *Yorkshire Post* and many other papers have been lost. One which we had sent, by Howard Spring in *Country Life,* ended with the words 'A model of what a guide book should be'. We were kept busy signing copies at W H Smiths and other bookshops. Smiths gave up their main windows to displays with a large blown-up photograph of the frontispiece — a watercolour of Kettlewell. Dents were pleased, and the book sold well.

Many friends and many strangers from far afield wrote appreciative letters. H L Bradfer-Lawrence said 'You have contributed a lasting factual, historical development of the area and its people'. Vera Hutton Croft, whose family were friends of Joan's and who was the daughter of Walter Morrison, had given the Malham Tarn estate for a Field Study Centre. She wrote to Joan expressing her pleasure at reading the book, and told her that 'James Morrison bought Malham Tarn for his son, Walter, and gave each of his sons a place, on condition that they were all to be in a different county, or they would quarrel. The only two who were near each other, South Hampshire and Wiltshire, were not on speaking terms.'

Dorothy Una Ratcliffe, then living in Edinburgh, sent letters saying 'It's a lovely loveable book'. Our friend, John Lawrence, still in the army, wrote from Celle, Germany, 'I am simply amazed by the amount of research that you must have done, and the quantity of material collected, assimilated and finally selected', Nellie McNeil O'Farrell, our agent at the Public Record Office, thanked us for being sent a copy of the book and praised the illustrations. Maurice Beresford sent congratulations, and Edgar Routh, a member of an ancient Wensleydale family and an agent at Reuters, wrote many long letters. Another (in 1958) came from a prisoner at HM Prison, Northallerton, where our friend George Jackson, amongst his many other activities, taught art. Evidently George had asked us to send this man a copy through the Governor. No-one could have written a better thank you, well put and well written.

The book was reprinted by Dents in 1960, and brought out as an Aldine paperback in 1963 at 7s. It was noticed in very many papers together with other paperbacks, and advertised by Dents in the company of Conrad and Dylan Thomas. As some said, at that price it was remarkable value considering the work involved. It was frequently reprinted with different jackets, and in 1991 was issued by Smith Settle in a larger format, so that it is still in print forty years on.

IN THE PUBLIC EYE

On 10th November 1960, at the invitation of the Lord Mayor of Leeds, we attended a literary luncheon at the Civic Hall. Over twenty Yorkshire authors were present, amongst them Stan Barstow, Phyllis Bentley, John Braine, Lettice Cooper, David Storey and Leo Walmsley. John Braine remarked, 'If a bomb dropped on this table there would be precious little modern literature worth reading'. The luncheon was recorded by ABC Television as the first in a series entitled 'The Bookman', and was shown on 20th November.

At this luncheon the editor of the *Yorkshire Post*, Kenneth Young, presided, with John Betjeman next to him as an important guest. Newly appointed, it was Kenneth Young who started the Yorkshire Post Literary Luncheons. He told us that he proposed to start a series of short articles of about 350 words on the countryside, and eventually asked us by letter to be the first contributors. He added 'I have enjoyed — and indeed, possess all your books'.

The series was to be called 'Country and Coast'. After a delay we began it on 1st April 1961, and continued apart from one or two exceptions until 7th March 1967, in all 164 pieces. They appeared sometimes weekly, sometimes at longer intervals, and for subject matter embraced farming, birds, flowers, walks, weather, seasonal sights

Marie and Joan at a literary luncheon.

Semerwater in winter.

and topical matters. Our contributions were usually headed 'Upper Wensleydale', signed M H and J I, and adorned with a small drawing changed fairly often, supplied by Marie. Later a staff artist took over.

At first plenty of material lay at hand, but as time went on we were kept constantly on the lookout. We made use of walks, encounters, and news from farming friends. Looking back now, writing these pieces was a pleasurable experience, and they remind us of a different world and forgotten activities. Some are run-of-the-mill, some quite charming, and some unique. A few readers told us that they enjoyed following us about, and indeed they read in a way like a diary. Here are a few excerpts from 'Country and Coast'. The second, on 25th April 1961, reads:

> Great efforts are being made and rightly so for the eradication of smoke from towns. In the remote Yorkshire Dales smoke remains what it has always been, a sign of habitation. On a bright still day in spring you can see several miles up and down the dale, each village pinpointed by its little cloud of smoke that is constantly augmented, yet constantly thinning, as it rises and floats gently down the valley ... Just by looking at the chimneys you can roughly forecast the weather, tell the time, and guess what your neighbours are doing.

Semerwater often drew us to its shores, for its prehistory and legend of a doomed village, its early Quaker history, and its rare birds and flora. At the end of January 1962 we sent in the following:

> It was a sunny day ... the lake lay partially entrapped in ice, and with the waters of melting snow flooding the margins ... On the west side we espied ten or fifteen little birds so tame that we were able to encircle them and through glasses obtain a close-up of what turned out to be a party of siskins and lesser redpolls. It was one of the most charming ornithological sights we have ever seen.

Smoke over Askrigg village.

On 3rd Novembers 1962,we found ourselves at Cherry Cobb Sands in Holderness, to us a faraway place that we had never visited before.

Driving along narrow straight roads, we saw no other vehicles . Just as people used to wave to the trains, so men working in the fields waved to us as we passed. At intervals we saw fine large farmsteads and much activity in the extensive ploughed fields. In one eight or ten women were picking potatoes; in another four men were harrowing. Two were using caterpillar tractors, necessary here because of the 'strong' heavy land. Sandbanks at Stone Creek, on to which a few boats had been drawn up, enclosed a narrow inlet, with in the background a dull red-brick farmhouse.

Our contributions to 'Country and Coast' gradually petered out, and finished for the time being on 7th March 1969. But the series continued, eventually in a much larger format, and lastly we were invited to send three more sketches in 1989, and wrote on Gordale, Hubberholme and Hawes.

In those days W T Oliver was deputy editor and art critic of the *Yorkshire Post*, and he passed on our 'Country and Coast' articles to Bernard Dineen, the features editor.We remember the help that Mr Dineen gave us with reviews when he became literary editor, and, as we write in 1995, his Monday column with candid comments on topical subjects still appears in the paper.

W T Oliver, deputy editor of the Yorkshire Post *(1939-1968).*

We knew Mr Oliver, who had a cottage at Starbotton over in Wharfedale, well, and must pay tribute to his friendship, his courtesy, and his work for the Brontë Society. His regime at the *Yorkshire Post* benefitted many people connected with the arts. He retired in 1968, and a letter, written in reply to one of ours, is typical of his generosity. He said: 'I admire your books which have always seemed to me models of their kind and a lasting service to the true appreciation of Dales life and landscape'.

As well as short pieces, we wrote several feature articles for the paper, such as 'A

Pioneer of Medicine', 'Summer in the Dales', 'All the Fun of the Show', 'New Light on Dotheboys Hall', 'Threat to Dales Houses', and 'The Past come to Life'. The last referred to a farmhouse kitchen set up in Bolton Castle by four dalesfolk, Margaret Hopper, George Jackson, Kit Calvert and Jim Peacock, with the approval of Lord Bolton. Some of these feature articles were included in a *Yorkshire Post* anthology called *The Bed Post* published in 1962. Now and again Mr Oliver sent us a book to review, chief of which was the Pevsner *North Riding* in the buildings of England series.

Although we suffered from nerves and never professed to be good public speakers, we did take trouble in preparing lectures, and gave slide shows (which we enjoyed) to many groups. We attended as guest authors a *Yorkshire Post* Literary Luncheon at the Queen's Hotel, Leeds, in 1965, and took a few Askrigg friends with us. The following year we were speakers at a similar luncheon at Hull, and later in 1972 a highlight was a Halloween dinner attended by members of the Yorkshire aristocracy. Ghost stories were the theme. Is it boastful to quote Richard Douro, who organised these *Yorkshire Post* events? He wrote 'You are one of Yorkshire's biggest assets ... You are good for literature, good for Yorkshire and good for the literary luncheons'. At least our egos, never very pronounced, were boosted.

In July 1964 we were asked to speak at the annual meeting of the Ryedale branch of the Council of Preservation of Rural England, at Gilling Castle, where we met many friends. In January 1966 we gave a slide show to the Farmers Discussion Group at Hawes. Afterwards, a farmer who we knew well came up, and said that he had not expected to enjoy it, but he had. We remember in 1969 Mr Oliver asking us to speak at a dinner of the Chippendale Society at Otley, where the cabinet-maker was born. Marie sat next to Mr Oliver's wife, Wyn, with whom she became engrossed in lively conversation, so that when she rose to speak her voice had almost gone.

We enjoyed lecturing twice to a group of West Riding librarians at Wakefield, and we once went to Hebden Bridge. Here we had given them a choice of subjects, and at the end of the talk, they sadly said that they had chosen the wrong one, and would we go again. We spoke to several branches of the Association of Yorkshire Bookmen, and at one at Morley a dire fatality occurred. After the talk Marie placed her box of slides on top of the roof of the car, forgot all about them, and drove off. In spite of returning to try to find them, advertising in Yorkshire papers, and contacting the police, they never turned up. It was a loss from which we never recovered. They were our best slides.

We have already mentioned an article on 'Lead-Mining Country' published in *Country Life* magazine in October 1948. This was followed in 1950 by 'Two Great Westmorland Fairs'. These were Appleby and Brough Hill Fairs, which we visited annually if we could, and had taken suitable photographs at a time when the gypsy caravans were being replaced by motorised vehicles. These articles were secondary and not prominent features of the magazine, but were appreciated by the editor, John Adams, who once wrote saying that he had not had anything from us lately. Written at intervals, the last of our nine articles for *Country Life*, 'Remembering a Farmhouse Relic' (cheese presses), appeared in April 1980.

We have spoken of what we call 'Coleshouse Days', and here is one for 24th March 1965:

> It was Dick's [Dick Chapman's] seventieth birthday. At 9.45 we took him an oil painting, done last December, of the river. He seemed delighted. We went on and collected Mrs Hopper and returned to Bolton Castle. Made notes for an article for the *Yorkshire Post* and Hare [photographer from Leyburn] came and took a photograph. Back at about 12. Went to luncheon club, and as it was an artist painting a portrait in oils — Mrs Cummins, I had to propose the vote of thanks. Home and wrote article on Kitchen [at Bolton Castle]. Had supper and went to Parish Council Annual meeting, followed by committee meeting. A lot of business, Christmas tree, lighting church, cobbles, Parish Council power, charities and our application for a way over the green.

In May of that year, J B Priestley and his wife, Jacquetta, stayed at the Rose and Crown at Bainbridge in order for him to write an article on the Yorkshire Dales for *Life International*. Some of his paintings illustrated it. In September, Lettice Cooper stayed with us for the night, as she was speaking to the Wensleydale Ladies Luncheon Club, and had to be ferried around. It was in fact a very happy visit. We ourselves gave the talk at the first luncheon club.

In 1966 Joan Bostock of the Association of Agriculture in London asked us to help with 'A Farm in the Yorkshire Dales', one of sample studies of individual farms. The scheme was linked with Leeds University and Harwood Long of the Agricultural Department, who we knew well. First she had to decide on the farm, and she chose Lowlands at Askrigg, farmed by R M (Dick) Hodgson. Dick, his wife and family were friends, and indeed Marie painted a picture of the farmhouse for a presentation for Dick's sixtieth birthday. We wrote two of the many sections, one of 4,000 words on the 'Historical Background' and the other a shorter piece on 'Wensleydale Cheese'. The bulk of the information was provided by Dick. The result was a comprehensive account of Lowlands in loose sheets in a strong folder — a valuable study of a Dales farm. Just before publication Joan Bostock arrived, displeased with us because her scrutineers at London University had challenged our statement that corn had been grown in Wensleydale. We persuaded her that we were correct, and she subsided.

In 1965, Marie had celebrated her sixtieth birthday, the age of retirement, and Joan a little behind, was fifty-four. That year, far from retirement, we began *Life and Tradition in the Yorkshire Dales* as our diaries record with almost daily sorties all over the Dales, continued with *Life in the Moorlands of North-East Yorkshire*, and *Life and Tradition in West Yorkshire*, a stint of eleven years.

A FAMOUS GUEST

J B Priestley stayed with us as a guest from the 8th to the 19th September, 1962. This came about for three reasons — his wife Jacquetta, was away at a conference in Canada; he was commissioned to write an article on the Yorkshire Dales for the *Sunday Times* Colour Supplement, and he wished to have a painting holiday. He first approached his friend of long standing, Phyllis Bentley, who felt physically not up to looking after, feeding and transporting him around the county, so she suggested that we be asked to house him as a guest. We exchanged letters, and on 29th August he ended one with: 'I shall probably fill your nice neat house with confusion, tobacco smoke, and the smell of rye whisky, but shall do my best to be a quiet respectable lodger.' At that time we were not total strangers, as we had visited him before at his home near Stratford-upon-Avon when writing *Yorkshire Portraits* and had established a rapport. After all we, too, were Yorkshire born and bred.

Apparently J B, as we were instructed to call him, was not mechanically minded, and was too preoccupied with other matters to drive a car, so his secretary brought him to Skipton, where we met him. He was wearing a flat wide-brimmed hat, but later exchanged it for a Basque beret. He also wore his rather lank hair slightly long at the back. We were naïvely surprised that such a well-established famous man should choose to adopt a slightly Bohemian appearance. He was particularly fond of the beret.

J B Priestley painting at Ribblehead.

We were not in the least apprehensive at the prospect ahead. We were the hosts, and knew what was to be our role. Nor did we want any payment, but without giving us a chance to refuse, J B had arranged by letter that he was to pay us £5 a day for everything. As he was being paid a large sum for his article, it seemed a fair deal. Priestley was a generous man in many directions. We established him in our large bedroom, which pleased him, and supplied him with a table for his typewriter. One can see how he managed such a huge output of essays, novels and plays; for he typed directly on to a sheet of paper without the need for drafts or corrections. What a flow of ideas in lively prose burst forth from him spontaneously. He told us that he was easily bored, hence his constant zest for living and for work. 'I have enjoyed hopping from one field to another, even if it meant missing some of the harvest'.

Every morning about 10.00 am he was waiting at the door with his painting satchel. We had to be up early because J B disdained sandwiches and we had to bake pies. He also refused camp chairs for picnics, and preferred to sit on a rug on the ground. During the week we toured many of the dales with the aim of finding suitable views for him to paint. At first, for two or three days we were dogged by a *Sunday Times* press photographer, who had his own car and followed us. Unfortunately the weather let us down. The photographer became frustrated and a bit bad-tempered, until at Hubberholme we directed him to a track above the church where he took a photograph of his quarry to his liking. As J B said with experience, these photographers wanted original pictures like back views out of focus.

On these expeditions we went for walks, whilst J B painted views of Ingleborough, Pen-y-Ghent, Tan Hill Inn, and vistas of Dentdale, Littondale and Malhamdale. He painted in gouache, occasionally using his finger, and yellow was a favourite colour. He told us 'I always exaggerate a little'. His bold, likeable pictures only lacked draughtsmanship. He plainly loved this hobby, and shone with satisfaction after a painting session. About twelve was a good haul for a week's work. One day we attended the Swaledale Agricultural Show at Muker, where a photographer from a local paper soon recognised him. Another day we organised an outing to catch crayfish in the River Ure[1], and to do so introduced him to our friend, Dick Chapman, retired schoolmaster and water bailiff. J B found Dick 'a man after his own heart'. His real work, the article for *The Sunday Times*, was typed in between returning home and dinner.

At night after we had had dinner, J B smoked his pipe, and entertained us with talk, or we listened to records or watched television. At that time we were fortunate in having help with the cooking, and with this capable assistance we rang the changes each night. We boiled our crayfish (never again), and made a delicious quiche which was seriously considered and judged to have slightly too thick a crust! When we had chicken, J B chose a leg, saying we must remember that he was a family man. For one night our butcher produced a rack of lamb, a joint that we had never had before and have never had since. For drinks our guest had brought with him a bottle of his

[1] Crayfish are today very scarce in the River Ure.

favourite Canadian rye whisky. He did suffer from gout, but assured us that this was not owing to over-consumption of alcohol.

When later in the week, on 13th September, it was J B's birthday, he proposed a celebratory dinner at the Red Lion at Burnsall in Wharfedale, and when he telephoned there, he was hard-pressed to find a dish that we had not had. The receptionist suggested Hungarian goulash, to which he replied 'Leave goulash to the Hungarians' (we had smoked salmon and duck). Wine flowed and strong coffee was consumed. Joan drove home, whilst J B and Marie sang old songs and operatic arias.

He was pleased to find that we had a number of his books, including a well-worn copy of *The Good Companions*, and, which pleased him far more, *Literature and Western Man*, recently published in 1960. It is well known that literary critics classed him as a popular novelist, of which he disapproved, even though *The Good Companions* started him on his way to wealth. Nor was he particularly proud of his wartime broadcasts, 'spoken essays, designed to have a very broad and classless appeal'. *Literature and Western Man* is a tour de force, showing the breadth and scope of his reading from university days onwards. We also had the books of autobiographical essays: *Midnight in the Desert* (1940), *Delight* (1949), *Margin Released* (1962) and the sometimes prophetic *Thoughts in the Wilderness* (1957). The latter is worth reading today for a forecast of change, a new society, a different middle class, writers ignored and the influence of television ('Vision has been replaced by television'). J B offered to sign our books, saying that he only did so for friends. Not for him the free-for-all of book signing sessions. His spidery sloping signatures plus 'for Marie Hartley and Joan Ingilby' decorate the title pages.

J B assumed that we were well read, and remarked on our set of Trollope's novels. But we could not compete with his musical knowledge. 'We in England', he declared 'don't have enough of innocent pleasures — not enough music, for instance, available for all'. He told us of the wonderful concerts held in his house on the Isle of Wight. 'Three things keep a man alive', he said on another occasion, 'ideas, art (any form of art) and nature. If you are not interested in any of these you die. Everybody should do something creative'. Once he recommended that we watch a boxing match on television, and proceeded to offer a running commentary.

We remember sitting, on the ground of course, for a picnic by Kirk Bridge near Dent Town. He began talking about time which had a fascination for him, and Dunne's *Experiment with Time*. His plays *Time and the Conways* and *I Have Been Here Before* are witness to this interest. Once he dilated on Jung, whom he had met and who he preferred to Freud — this led to an exposition of Jung's psychology in relation to the archetypal figure and creative work, ideas at that time very much to the fore. On another occasion he enquired whether we had experienced pure happiness coming from nowhere and without obvious cause. Women, he thought, had too much humility and were less different from men in capabilities and temperaments than commonly supposed.

We did not always agree with his opinions, but refrained from argument. For instance he told us that as topographers and social historians we were in the wrong sphere of literature, and we should change. We let this pass, as we enjoy our work, the research, the recording of oral tradition leading to the discovery of new facts. Novels and biographies certainly dominate the literary scene. But we sometimes wonder about the fate of some of the novels lengthily reviewed, and suspect that they will sink with very little trace, whereas some of our books dating from the 1930s and 1950s are still in print, and a good number command high prices in antiquarian bookshops. Only recently we priced one, *The Charm of Yorkshire Churches*, published at 5s in 1935 and now costing £35. J B also averred that writing about a place far away from the reality was easier, such as writing about England in Arizona, and in fact when Ella Pontefract and Marie moved from Wetherby to Askrigg in Wensleydale, Ella found that she had to adjust to writing about a place near at hand.

J B started life as a socialist, but hinted that the huge tax demands of the Labour Party had caused him to rethink. He was, he told us, offered a peerage, but could not see himself in that role, so refused it. Also he and his family had enjoyed many holidays. Recently, together with their domestic staff, they had spent one in Amalfi. He spoke of Samarkand, remembered because he was so ill there, and he thought that the Grand Canyon in Arizona was *the* wonder of the world. He explained that he had had to visit Russia in order to spend roubles earned there, as they were not allowed out of the country. Of his love for the Yorkshire Dales, he wrote in the article for the *Sunday Times*: 'I have never seen more beautiful, more satisfying, more rewarding country than that of the Yorkshire Dales'. Explaining to us why he did not live there, he pointed out that he had to live near London. This we are sure was true. The Dales are extremely inconvenient for quick travel to the capital. Few people attain all their fondest wishes and desires.

In 1957 the divorce of Jacquetta and Christopher Hawkes had gone through, and in 1962 J B was still smarting at the unfairness of the judge's remarks at the trial. It so happened that we knew the Hawkes, as they had stayed at Askrigg with their son Charles in 1948. We showed them archaeological remains, and Jacquetta went fishing. Marie remembers a conversation in 1962 whilst sitting with J B in the George at Hubberholme waiting for Joan and the press photographer to arrive. 'I've had a lot of sex' he remarked, and Marie, a spinster, wondered for a second how to respond. But there was no need. He was only reminiscing. He once said that women liked him. They liked his warm hands. As has been said elsewhere, the marriage to Jacquetta, his third wife, was a very happy one.

The visit came to an end. The party was over. He wrote in our visitor's book: 'And everything was perfect except for the weather.' Just once he was unnecessarily rude on the occasion of a casual meeting, and we were half-angry, half-sorry that he could behave like that. He suggested that if we wished, we write an article on his visit to Yorkshire for the *Yorkshire Post*, which we did. We took him beyond Huddersfield to meet his secretary who had driven up from Stratford. He asked us to visit him at his flat in Albany in London at Kissing Tree House near Stratford, which again we did. At Stratford he showed us some of his pictures of the Dales which he had had framed. He once said that he and Jacquetta wondered whether they would afford to go on living in this mansion with its indoor and outdoor staff, but as it turned out his plays

Hubberholme, where J B's ashes are scattered.

were being performed all over the world in many languages. Hardly a day went by without a performance somewhere, and royalties flowed in. He enjoyed and was proud of his fine home. It had been a long journey from the house in a Bradford street, where he was born of lower middle class parents (his classification), to Kissing Tree House.

Also, in later years, driven by Jacquetta, he came a few times to the Dales. One episode merits recording. At Askrigg they had walked down the pastures north of the village instead of walking down the road, and they arrived at our house to say that they had lost the car keys! We rushed to our local garage, but of course no-one had an ignition key for a Mercedes Benz, and in the end Jacquetta set forth again retracing her steps down the pastures and found them.

Priestley died in 1984, and his ashes were buried in the churchyard at Hubberholme, and a plaque placed to his memory on a column in the church. By then we had lost touch. Towards the end of his life he could no longer bemoan, as he was wont to do, the lack of praise and appreciation accorded authors including himself, especially by Yorkshire folk. In the 1970s he was given the Order of Merit, the Freedom of the City of Bradford, and an honorary doctorate at Bradford University. In 1986 a statue of him was erected in the city, and in 1994, the centenary of his birth, around 13th September (the day we had gone with him on the jaunt to Burnsall in 1962), exhibitions, books and articles paid tribute to his life and achievements.

ASKRIGG ART CLUB

In the early 1960s it became known that we had a collection of slides from art galleries in England and abroad, and also that Marie had studied art history at the Slade School in London. There she had attended lectures given by Professor Tancred Borenius, and on Saturday mornings had returned to the Slade to go through the school's collection of slides to familiarise herself with great pictures. Now, it is taken for granted that one recognises great paintings, but for the student much was strange and new, and had to be learnt.

Except for professional artists, such as Fred Lawson, the practice of visual art in Wensleydale, or knowledge of great artists and the history of European painting, were virtually unknown. The bias of culture in the dale lay in music; the choral societies, orchestras, brass bands and the Wensleydale Tournament of Song, held every spring, were long established and pre-eminent. Also Yorebridge Grammar School, then at Askrigg, and very much a part of life in the upper dale, had neither a trained art teacher nor an art department.

By the early 1960s we had brought back slides after visits to galleries in Italy and Holland, the Louvre in Paris, and the National and the Tate Galleries in London. We found France, apart from the Louvre, lacking in choice, whilst in Italy, treasuring its artistic heritage, slides were available in every gallery and often in churches. We remember going to a small hill-top town, Cordoba, in Italy, where a church had a Fra Angelico, and, what is more, slides of it. On a later visit to Italy, reaching Ravenna, we were able to buy superb slides of the mosaics, and in 1964, visiting Madrid, we brought slides home from the Prado. So when requests came for lectures, we had the means and also the enthusiasm.

At Yorebridge, for a year or two, taking three periods a term, and with the compliance of Donald Brisbane, the headmaster, Marie gave illustrated lectures on European art to sixth form students. Also she and Joan presented a prize of a framed print for the best art work at the school. Eventually this lapsed for want of entries. Once in July 1962, we attended a lecture at the school on 'Portraiture' given by four girls and a boy and based on a filmstrip, followed by a discussion. This was heartening.

In addition, Marie was invited to take classes for the Workers Educational Association at Askrigg, and also at Leyburn. In the autumn of 1962 she began with twelve lectures at Askrigg, starting with an 'Introduction to European Painting: Giotto to Picasso', and ending with 'Modern Art; Cubism, Abstract, Surrealism, Expressionism' It was a difficult time as her mother was failing, and died in January 1963. Once she gave a lecture to the Wensleydale Society on European Art, but on this occasion, wishing to make the most of the opportunity, put too much in.

Early in January 1965, one of those who had attended these classes, Michael Weatherald, the local builder, came up to our house to discuss the formation of an art group, and as a result a meeting was held on 25th January in the Temperance Hall,

Askrigg, which attracted twenty-five people. It was agreed to form the Askrigg Art Club, and officers were appointed — Michael, chairman, Rita Craske, secretary, Barbara Widdows, treasurer. Officially we were elected presidents, but in reality Marie was the tutor. A small committee consisting of officers and a few members was appointed to arrange programmes in future years. It was decided that we should meet fortnightly on Thursdays, and that there should be two classes of membership, one for drawing, limited in numbers, and paying £1 annually, and the other lecture members, unlimited in numbers, paying 10s. Thus the Askrigg Art Club started in a flush of enthusiasm, initiated by local people, and so it grew and flourished for sixteen years.

We started off by meeting in the primary school, but as some members took up oil painting which needed more space, we moved to the back room of the Temperance Hall. At first Marie and Joan provided still-lifes as subjects, but later members took this in turn. For the first class on 11th February 1965, twenty-three drawing members were present. In March, as we were leaving on a Greek cruise, we enlisted the help of our friend George Jackson, who came as tutor in our absence. Each fortnight Marie went round the class, giving advice and help where necessary. Silence prevailed and when a naturally talkative person joined, she soon learnt to keep quiet. Talent varied, but everyone enjoyed themselves, and occasionally the least talented brought off a worthwhile study. In the summer we worked out of doors at different venues, such as Semerwater, gardens, bridges and hillsides. Often minutes record disappointment with the weather.

Sometimes we had demonstrations, and sometimes a professional artist took the class. In 1974, Janet Rawlins gave us an evening on her speciality, 'Collage'. Rita Busby demonstrated 'Landscape in Pastel'. Angus Rands, then a prominent watercolourist much sought after, painted a picture of Appletreewick in front of us out of his head, and to achieve his own fresh style used quantities of water, throwing paint water into a bucket.

Two, sometimes three lectures took place in the year, all of a high standard, A true friend of the club, Helen Kapp, keeper of Abbot Hall Gallery at Kendal, came four times, once giving a lecture with slides on Stubbs, which she had just delivered at galleries in New York. W T Oliver, deputy editor of the *Yorkshire Post* and art critic, spoke on the 'Romanticism of English Art', and refused the fee offered, saying that he approved of art clubs. Peter Walton of Temple Newsam introduced us to Leeds pottery, and another lecturer took Munch as his subject. Fred and Muriel Lawson and Sonia (now a Royal Academician) came for an evening, bringing many beautiful paintings to show us. Once we were looking forward to a lecture on 'Flower Painting' by Sybil Cole, who rushed this through, in order to talk on Fred Elwell, artist of Beverley, thus giving us two lectures in one night. Sometimes we borrowed films from the British Film Institute or the Arts Council. One with Sir Kenneth Clarke attracted a large audience, but the soundtrack inclined to boom. Towards the end J C Medley spoke on the Barber Institute at Birmingham, with which his family were closely connected. From time to time, especially at the beginning, Marie filled in, with for instance a lecture on Goya after the visit to Madrid.

An Askrigg Art Club evening class near Yore Bridge.

The highlights of those years were the often ambitious annual outings, usually by bus, driven by our local garage proprietor, but also by train. We remember members one by one gathering on the platform at Northallerton Station in the cold of the early morning to board a train for London, where in 1969 we visited the National Gallery, had a meal in the café, and went on to the Queen's Gallery which was showing drawings by Leonardo Da Vinci. On these outings, seats on trains had to be booked and meals for a party arranged by our secretary, Rita Craske, who never failed us. Rita had the gift of creating a happy atmosphere and we co-operated with her in complete accord. A second visit to London to the Tate Gallery was marred by torrential rain, and the resultant scarcity of taxis. We shepherded some of our flock on to buses, and all reached Kings Cross safely for the homeward journey.

In 1973 we went by train to Edinburgh to see the National Gallery of Scotland and the Museum of Modern Art, then in the Botanic Gardens. At the National Gallery we were taken behind the scenes and shown precious watercolours by Turner and others, kept in portfolios. Some members finished up by shopping in Marks and Spencer in Princes Street.

But our greatest adventure was the day's outing to Glasgow, made possible by sixteen of us motoring to Oxenholme station near Kendal on the west coast route. Boarding the train, we found no reserved seats and were stranded in the corridor. However, our secretary had the letter confirming the booking, and we were ushered into first-class compartments. At Glasgow, apologies to Askrigg Art Club were relayed over the tannoy. Our first call was at Pollock House, then the precursor of the Burrell Collection, where we had lunch in a huge kitchen with gleaming copper pans.

The Art Club Christmas party, 1973.

The Askrigg Art Club annual outing in 1979 to Pollock House, Glasgow.

Taxis, arranged for us by the curators, took us on to Kelvingrove Art Gallery and its splendid collections.

Outings were always well supported. One of the first was to Abbot Hall at Kendal, others to Wakefield and Bradford Art Galleries, to Durham Cathedral and the Gulbenkian Museum nearby, as well as several great houses. One outing to Cropper's Paper Mill at Burneston near Kendal was the outcome of a friendship between one of the workers and his admiration for the Hartley/Ingilby books. We saw the processes of paper-making from tanks of porridge-like sludge to quality paper emerging at the end, and we were presented with samples of their products.

Finally, as the climax of the year, a Christmas party was organised in the back room of the Temperance Hall. Michael Weatherald lent huge white boards which, propped on tables round the walls, made splendid screens for fixing on pictures with Blu-Tack. We all subscribed to a faith supper, notable for the almost professional cooking of some members. Dressed in our best, we sat at small tables whilst Marie went round the pictures one by one hinting at improvements, praising many, and approving pride in the year's work. It was far and away the best village party we ever attended, but then we were biased.

In 1980, although the club had in all fifty-three members, after sixteen years it came to an end. Other art classes had started. Possibly we had shot our bolt. In the event all the officers resigned, one or two for reasons of health, and no-one offered to take our places. The secretary had given her services throughout. Michael had opted for other interests, and Professor T B Worth had taken his place, and Margaret Peacock was then treasurer. It was decided to wind up the funds (£97) by paying for a party at Riverdale Country House Hotel at Bainbridge. At this event Rita Craske was presented with a framed aquatint of Coverham Abbey, which a former member had donated to the club; Joan was given a bouquet; and Marie a large album containing original work by the drawing members, compiled by Janet Rawlins. Since then the club has enjoyed an annual reunion party at Riverdale, organised by Janet, with a buffet supper, followed by a lecture by Marie. Occasionally others — Enid Moore, Fred Willis and John Hill — spoke on Australian art, watercolours and Matisse. This event lasted until 1994, twenty-nine years since the start.

A few members continued to meet informally, and four still meet in each other's homes to paint a still-life, and in summer to work out of doors. As for Yorebridge Grammar School, it no longer functions as such, and at the Wensleydale School, which now serves the whole dale at Leyburn, an art department and an art master form part of the curriculum.

Many of us look back on the club with pleasure, and often share recollections. For us, although it had to be fitted in with work, it was one of the happiest and most enjoyable activities of our lives. It would not have occurred to us at the time, but looking back, we feel gratified that we were able to give our talents, such as they were, to a community that has offered us so much.

A TRIO OF BOOKS

The year 1957 proved to be an important one for us, in that we built on a large room at the back of the house, intended to be a workroom. Up to then one of us had worked in a spare bedroom, originally Marie's studio, and the other in the dining-room — all inconvenient. We engaged an architect from Kendal who drew up plans, and then the local builders, Thomas Weatherald and Son, took over. Michael had just returned from war service. The architect suggested clerestory windows looking up to a hillside pasture, where sheep still graze to our perpetual delight. At the end of May the first parquet floor ever undertaken by the firm was being laid. A long range of bookshelves and cupboards accommodated our books, art materials, photographic equipment and so on. When all was finished, friends asked: 'How did you manage before?'

On 29th August 1957 we flew from London to Amsterdam, taking Marie's niece, Brenda, with us, to see the art galleries of Holland. It was a particularly happy visit, because the Dutch people, noting that we were English and remembering our part in the war, could not have been more welcoming. We visited the Ryksmuseum twice, saw *The Nightwatch*, Rembrandt's house, and spent two days at the Hague and at Haarlem. An ambitious outing took us by bus and train to the Kröller Müller Museum where famous Van Goghs were then to be seen, and to an Open Air Museum at Arnhem. As good luck would have it, a group of elderly Dutch men and women in Dutch costume were there on an outing. The women's white lawn caps with many tiny pleats were particularly charming. The older farmhouses, incorporating the barns under one roof, were huge and lofty. Some Dutch friends once told us that if there

Marie and Joan in the new room, built in 1957. In fact we work at separate tables at either end of the room.

was a thunderstorm, the whole family, together with their most prized belongings, gathered in the middle of the structure. Our return flight was marred by a mix-up over the spelling of Joan's name. She, as Marie Hartley, and Brenda went off on the booked flight, and Marie had to follow as Joan Ingilby on the next. KLM compensated us, but we were very late for an appointment at Dents.

Meanwhile, during the summer of 1956 we had visited Haworth, and went on to Hebden Bridge at the head of Calderdale. As we motored down the long sloping road and came in sight of the town, we stopped to look at the ranks of terraced houses hugging the hillside. One of us said 'It's a wonder of Yorkshire', and the other replied, 'That's the name for a book'.

As usual, in January 1957 we consulted Dents by sending them three suggestions for books, one of them 'The Wonders of Yorkshire'. Bozzie wrote: 'It is an excellent idea, and I suggest that the illustrations should be made into a very strong feature'. Following the submission of a synopsis, we signed a contract with a completion date of 31st December 1958. From our point of view 'The Wonders of Yorkshire' was a good idea. Naturally the owners and custodians of historic buildings, businesses, coalmines, steel works, worsted mills, towns and cities with special features liked their charges being called wonders, so that ready co-operation resulted. Also some of the events to which we were given entry were privileged. However, as will appear in due course, this book might be described as accident-prone.

Our list of wonders numbered 100, and we spent the whole of 1958 hurrying from place to place. Again we took advantage of the hospitality of relatives. In May we were staying with Marie's mother at Scarborough, where we visited Whitby, Lastingham and Burton Agnes Hall. Permission both to visit and to make drawings had to be obtained beforehand. On 12th May we were at Leeds, whence we saw Temple Newsam, Nostell Priory and Harewood House. We stayed twice at the School Inn at Ackworth to see Conisbrough and Pontefract castles, and again, having made arrangements with the publicity officer of the National Coal Board, Donald Blythe, we went down Ledstone Luck Colliery. This was chosen as then the most modern pit in Yorkshire with the youngest manager. It was so called in 1911 when it was opened by the owner's wife wishing it luck. The experience of going down a mine as far as the coalface is described in the book. In 1986, at the time of the bitter strikes in the mining industry, Ledston Luck mine was closed and the site became an Enterprise Park.

In June, whilst staying with Joan's aunt at Ripley Castle, we visited Brimham Rocks and spent several days in York. In fact, we allocated to York ten wonders, most of which required pen-and-ink drawings. Marie entered in her diary 'June was quite horrific'. It included visits to Castle Howard, Beverley, Bempton Cliffs, York Assembly Rooms, Holme Moss Television Station and the Wool Exchange at Bradford. July proved nearly as bad. We went to Headingley Cricket Ground, Bolton Abbey and Farnley Hall to see the Turner watercolours of the house and of Wharfedale. Major Le G G Horton-Fawkes, a descendant of Walter Fawkes, friend of Turner, and his wife gave us lunch, so that this visit was one to remember. Later we went to

Harlow Carr Gardens at Harrogate, and the Great Yorkshire Show. After that visit the secretary sent us free tickets for the show for three following years.

In July we spent several days at a guest house in Kingston-upon-Hull with the sights of Holderness in mind, as well as Hull Docks and Hull Trinity House. At that time Hull ranked as one of the great ports of the world. We were issued by the dock police with an entrance permit, warned not to speak to anyone, and not to be lured on to any of the ships. From the roof of an office block, Marie drew trawlers belching forth oily black smoke, a splendid subject, but blackening both our faces. We were due to tea with the master warden of Hull Trinity House, and before going there repaired to public conveniences to wash our faces. Hull Trinity House is not open to the public, except for occasional visits by members of societies. The handsome interior, its ancient history, the navigational school, the connection with foreign parts and the courteous ships' captains who we met, made another outstanding experience.

A break from work occurred in August, a time for harvesting our fruit and vegetables, and also the annual visit of Marie's mother and aunt for a fortnight. Later we had a short holiday with Phyllis at Speech Houses in the Forest of Dean, seeing a play at Stratford on the way.

As both of us have happy childhood memories of the Grand Theatre at Leeds, it was naturally one of our wonders. John Beaumont, then the manager, co-operated willingly by allowing us to look all over the theatre, and then with difficulty by finding us seats in the dress circle for a performance of Handel's *Samson* by Covent Garden Opera Company in the presence of the Queen, glittering like a fairy princess. At the opening night of the theatre in 1878, the actor, Wilson Barrett, gave a speech. Marie's aunt once told us that she had seen Barrett in his play *The Sign of the Cross*, but had only been allowed to go to the theatre because it was a religious play. Much later we were privileged to hear and see a never-to-be-forgotten Wagner's *Ring* and many of the performances of Opera North.

Although we worked hard all the autumn, we again failed to meet our deadline, 31st December. Martin Dent issued dire warnings that we might miss publication in time for the Christmas sales. We had been allotted 320 pages, and in order to fit in as much as possible, we counted many of the texts to fill the pages without leaving wasteful gaps at the ends of each chapter, and as far as we remember made a paste-up for the book. Also we had submitted many of the wonders to the relevant heads of firms, secretaries, or public relations men to check for accuracy. Most were passed as correct, in some minor alterations were made, and in others a little information was added.

On 11th December Joan's mother died, and we both drove down to Ringwood in Hampshire to attend the funeral. Her mother had passed on to Joan many of her scholarly interests. On our return a message came from Marie's sister-in-law in Leeds that we had been sent tickets for the Christmas performance of *Messiah* to be given by the Huddersfield Choral Society (surely one of the wonders) in Huddersfield Town Hall. Sir Malcolm Sargent, who died in 1967, was the conductor. This again was never to be forgotten.

The line drawings, ready in early January, were sent off — some forty small drawings, forty full-page upright, and six double spreads. Bozzie wrote, 'Your most impressive collection of drawings which must represent a stupendous effort on your part. They are most varied and full of character'. Day after day spent drawing had given Marie opportunities for practice; for draughtsmanship requires constant practice. One of our favourite drawings was of Hebden Bridge from the Buttress, another Brodsworth Colliery with stooks of corn in the foreground, and a third a view of the Colne Valley crowded with mills and buildings. We remember, too, her drawing with permission at the River Don Works of English Steel at Sheffield, a dramatic

The Vale of York from Sutton Bank.

picture of a drop forge, which surprised the publicity man there in a city once very male-orientated. An equally dramatic double spread of Halifax from Beacon Hill, with smoke pouring from cooling towers and a myriad of mill chimneys, disturbed a few people in Halifax, then looking forward to Clean Air Acts and smokeless zones.

That year, 1959, letters shuttled backwards and forwards between us and Dents as production progressed. In May we were invited to lunch at the Authors Club by Bozzie at 'their restaurant to which ladies are invited'. Our host had to attend a memorial service, and was late, with the result that we were seated like pariahs in a prominent position to await his arrival. What we were likely to do we cannot imagine. Then, in July, a printers' strike, lasting for seven weeks, temporarily jeopardised publication in the autumn.

However, *The Wonders of Yorkshire* was published on 19th November 1959. Dents had two or three drawings blown up to poster size that made striking backgrounds for window displays in bookshops. Reviews in national and local newspapers were favourable, and reviewers treated us as well-known and established authors. Only one or two tried to score by choosing other wonders. The *Yorkshire Post* reviewer said 'It is all very satisfying, a symposium well worth having', and the *Huddersfield Examiner* described the book as 'a notable addition to the literature of Yorkshire'. The book sold well, and there was talk of a second edition.

In the January number of the *Dalesman*, Dr A and Mrs S R Raistrick reviewed the book and disparaged every aspect of it. So anxious were they to condemn that they mistakenly assumed that the little bridge at Hebden Bridge was the wonder, whereas we had made it plain that it was the town itself. Nor was mention made of the drawings, an integral part of the scheme of the book. It is of course a fact that such attacks do more harm to the writers than to the object of their disapproval. Harry Scott, the editor, could have and should have suppressed such a review, and we learnt then that loyalty to friends and supporters went by the board. Many people wrote protesting at the unfairness both to us and to the *Dalesman,* and Bozzie brushed it off, saying such things do happen. However, the diatribe damaged the sales of the book, and all thoughts of a second edition were dropped.

In 1969, ten years later, we heard from the editorial department at Dents that they were thinking of publishing a paperback edition of *The Wonders of Yorkshire.* Naturally we were at first pleased, and then realised how much had altered. We began again checking with a view to the publication of a revised edition. However, so much had changed in that short time. In the coalfields of South Yorkshire, uneconomic pits were being closed, mechanisation had increased the output, and oil, natural gas and nuclear power spelt a multi-fuel economy. The nationalisation of steel had altered the whole of steel production in the county, and a letter warned us that 'without a considerable amount of re-writing your reprint will be out of date before it is published'. The container revolution in the fishing industry had taken place, and the clothing industry was altogether differently organised.

Amongst other subjects, the *Yorkshire Post* had moved from Albion Street in Leeds, to ultra-modern premises in Wellington Street. Sir Linton Andrews had retired.

Marie and Joan sitting in the garden under the cherry tree, which grew too large and had to be cut down.

Harrogate could no longer be described as a spa, and at York Station the signal box was no longer the largest in England. Teesside had become a county borough, and Teesside Airport had opened for civilian use. In 1960, the Yorkshire Naturalists Trust had bought Spurn Peninsular. Even the names and numbers of the Cleveland Bays in the Royal Mews had altered. And so it went on page after page. We had hit off a short period of violent change.

However, we began to undertake the big task of revision and prepared many corrections that brought the book up-to-date. At first Dents thought that these were necessary, then gradually as costs started to be worked out, to include all our alterations, it was found to be impracticable. The offer was made that they would go forward if we would cut our alterations to a minimum, and when we declined to do so, they regretfully informed us that the book was not viable. We sometimes wonder whether we should have let the book go forward as it was as a paperback. It did record Yorkshire in its heyday.

During the summer of 1959, whilst we awaited the publication of *The Wonders of Yorkshire*, one of those brilliant spells of weather favoured us in the Dales. In those days a large cherry tree in the garden offered welcome shade, and a venue for al-fresco meals. Later in the year our friend Mrs Alderson of Stone House, upper Swaledale, asked us to keep her company whilst the members of her family went to Muker Show. It was very hot, and we all agreed that you could have fried an egg on the smooth flat stones of the garden wall. Stone House, which the Aldersons eventually left to farm it from the village of Keld, was known both to Ella Pontefract and to us as a haven of peace and goodwill.

On one of our visits to London, in a discussion at Dents, they put forward the idea of a sequel to *The Wonders* — a book on famous Yorkshire people. We thought it over and agreed, and eventually began making lists of people for possible inclusion. A scheme evolved whereby each famous person was to have a small drawing, the dates of their birth and death in the heading, and a short biography.

We started with Alcuin, theologian and educationalist, especially connected with the library at York in the eighth century, and finished with George Lascelles, Earl of Harewood, patron of music, in the twentieth century. The choice of men and women (hardly any women) in early centuries was easy, but, when it came to modern times, difficult decisions had to be made. To overcome this, we wrote a comprehensive introduction naming as many people as possible. As examples, there were then three famous scientists from Yorkshire, Fred Hoyle, Sir John Cockcroft and Sir Edward Appleton, and as for Yorkshire novelists we could only select three from a galaxy — J B Priestley, Phyllis Bentley and Winifred Holtby. (We were sorry not to include Lettice Cooper, whose novels we admired and who we knew.)

What emerged was the large number of outstanding personalities who were Yorkshire-born. This condition we took as our criterion, but perhaps two or three should not have been included, as although they were certainly born in Yorkshire, it was only because their parents had been temporarily domiciled in the county. In the end we chose sixty-eight, counting such families as the Brontës as one group.

For information we wrote to libraries, and here we must pay tribute to the great public libraries at Leeds, Bradford, Sheffield, Hull and York. We knew many of the librarians personally. We remember visiting Bradford without an appointment, and as the reference librarian had to go out, he offered us the use of his office and telephone. Mary Walton, then well-known, was in charge at Sheffield. We had a reader's ticket for Leeds, so that we could borrow there, and the York men sometimes lent us books. Many sent us lists of the famous people in their neighbourhood. When friends lent us their flat in Harrogate for five days, we visited many of the West Riding libraries. Besides information, they were often able to help with photographs, although we obtained many of these from the National Portrait Gallery. To make small drawings, Marie needed a photograph. Even when dealing with people we could visit, they would not have wanted to give up the time to pose for a portrait. Most of the drawings were successful and gave a good idea of the people concerned.

We wrote to all the living people, and in our zeal arranged interviews with several.

Our archives contain signed letters from J B Priestley, Vera Brittain, James Mason, Ian Carmichael, Leonard Hutton, Wilfred Pickles and Barbara Hepworth. We fitted in some of these appointments on our way to London or the south. Thus we met Priestley for the first time at his home near Stratford. When in time we sent the profile for him to check, he wrote: 'You have been far more accurate than most people who have tried their hand at this sort of thing with me'. In May a holiday was planned at St Ives, which gave us the opportunity to meet Barbara Hepworth at her studio there, and indeed we bought a small bronze 'Corymb'. She altered our script slightly and then pronounced it 'splendid'.

When we first wrote to Dame Edith Sitwell, she was ill, but her secretary suggested trying again when we were in London. We did so, but failed as Graham Greene was going to tea with her. James Mason sent delightful letters, and wrote that he was 'a tremendous admirer of *The Wonders of Yorkshire*'. We also had a rewarding correspondence with Grace Bentham, the daughter of Richard Kearton, who had died in 1928. He and his brother, Cherry, both famous naturalists, were born at Thwaite in Swaledale, where we still keep in touch with their relatives. Journeying from home, we met Sir Herbert Read at Stonegrave near Helmsley. We remember the visit with pleasure and we were shown all over the house.

On a trip to London in November 1961, we managed to see Lord Macintosh, Leonard Hutton, Wilfred Pickles, Henry Moore and Ian Carmichael, who we saw in his dressing room at the Savoy Theatre. Perhaps Leonard Hutton, obviously so much interviewed, so much praised, was the least interested. On the other hand, we went by train to Bishop Stortford to visit Henry Moore, and were shown his studios, and were given a personal conducted tour of a large paddock with massive figures placed here and there. After tea with him and his wife, a visiting American also there asked us to have dinner with him, but we had to refuse, having tickets for a play *The Mousetrap*. Moore liked his short biography and 'had read it with much pleasure'. One evening Eleanor Winthrop Young invited us to dinner at the Oxford University Club on Pall Mall.

Not all was work. Toward the end of June 1960, Bozzie and his daughter Emily (so called after Emily Brontë), came to stay for the weekend. We met them at Bradford Exchange Station, and drove to Haworth to the Parsonage. It was a full three days, including York to see the Minster, the Shambles, and in the afternoon the York Mystery Plays. On the Sunday we took them to Ripon, on to Fountains Abbey, and so to Harrogate Station for the return to London. Bozzie wrote that 'they had enjoyed every minute of it, not only the highlights but your company at your delightful cottage'. In September we were privileged to meet Arnold Toynbee at the Franklands at Needle House, Uldale, between Sedbergh and Kirkby Stephen. Both Dr Frankland and his daughter, Helga, wrote novels and expressed mutual interest in the Dales on our occasional meetings.

In August 1960 Marie illustrated *The Young Brontës*, a fictionalised version of their early lives by Phyllis Bentley in a series on 'Famous Childhoods'. It was interesting to find and to draw at the Castle Museum, York, some wooden soldiers of the right date and matching the description of those bought as a present for Branwell by Mr Brontë.

Working hard all the autumn of 1960, we were able to post the manuscript to Dents on 1st January 1961. Proofs arrived in June just before we left for a holiday at Wengen, Switzerland, where the alpine flowers were at their best. On 19th October, *Yorkshire Portraits* was published. Many and various reviews appeared in papers as far afield as the *Glasgow Herald*, the *Birmingham Post*, and the *Oxford Mail.* Although most were good, some complained that the biographies were too short, and others proposed different people. *The Times Literary Supplement* commented condescendingly that 'Although written on a fairly simple and naïve level, the book is not without interest'. Whereas the *Library Review* averred that 'There is a clearness and simplicity about the style of writing that makes *Yorkshire Portraits* particularly suitable for school and college libraries.' Sales were adequate, but it was not one of our bestsellers. Readers did not seem to subscribe to the view 'Let us all praise famous men'.

The book, *Getting to Know Yorkshire*, a children's book, occupied us from July 1962 to December 1963, a period of time filled with many other activities, pursuits and distractions. In May 1962 we spent a wonderful ten days in Italy based on Rome and Naples. In July, we had Phyllis Bentley to stay to recuperate from a near thrombosis, and, in September, J B Priestley came as described in the chapter devoted to his visit. We were writing articles for *Country Life* and the *Yorkshire Post*, including the regular contributions to 'Country and Coast'. Marie was giving WEA lectures on art, and beginning to paint oil paintings for commissions. For three years running we went to the Edinburgh Festival. Family visits continued, but in the autumn Marie's aunt fell ill and her mother was failing.

The idea for the children's book came about when a new traveller for Dents, Douglas Symington, took an interest in our work, and when we were undecided what to do after finishing *Yorkshire Portraits*, he had a talk with the head of the juvenile department at the West Riding Library headquarters in Wakefield, and was told that a children's book on Yorkshire was very much wanted. Others confirmed this view. The idea appealed to us, and Bozzie approved but asked for a synopsis, and warned that many people must be consulted as children's books were a specialised subject.

It almost goes without saying that we had accumulated a mass of material about the county to fall back on. Nonetheless we wrote to a great many officials who we knew at the National Coal Board, English Steel and so on. Again staying with relatives, we travelled round the county, from Scarborough going to Middlesbrough to see the ICI Wilton Works. Staying at hotels at Beverley and Driffield in the East Riding, we retraced some of our steps, and saw new places and buildings such as Sledmere House. We contacted a Mr Sutherland of the Ministry of Agriculture, and he introduced us to Mr and Mrs W W Gatenby of Littlethorpe, near Rudston, a large Wolds farm. We keep in touch with the Gatenbys to this day, and were significantly helped by them with our book *Yorkshire Album.*

Getting to know Yorkshire was well arranged, with individual chapters headed 'Going down a Coal-mine', 'A Visit to Bradford', 'A Tour of the Dales', 'Going round a Dales Farm', 'Looking at Abbeys', and so on. With the section on 'Early Man', we were helped by a friend, especially with a map of about 7,500 BC, hypothetical but based on research, showing the then landmass link between Yorkshire and the Continent. For the title page Marie drew the Folkton Drum, dating from the Beaker people of the Bronze Age, at the British Museum. Many maps and plans were drawn to clarify the text.

We also collected together twenty-nine photographs, of which sixteen were ours. A favourite was one taken in January 1937, of a flock of sheep gathered up on Grassington Moor. The figure of a farmer makes a focal point, whilst sheep with their fleeces encrusted with snow circle round him. We were helped by the son of farmer friends, Simon Hodgson, who was about to start a photographic course at college. He both took photographs and printed and enhanced some of ours. As a photographer, Marie regrets that she has never had time to develop and print her own films.

In January 1963, Bozzie was asking us to be patient about the book, as childrens' librarians and others must be consulted, but by the end of the month Dents agreed to the publication of a book to be called *Yorkshire for Children*, a title which in retrospect seems far better than *Getting to know Yorkshire* which replaced it. The contract was not signed until 3rd September 1963.

Meanwhile, we spent the Christmas of 1962 at Scarborough, and after a short spell at home were summoned back by the doctor, and on 20th January, Marie's mother died. She had always supported us in all our undertakings, and she was sadly missed. Marie's aunt stayed on in the family home until 1980, when she died aged ninety. A severe winter had already engulfed us, and on our return to Askrigg we had to shovel snow to reach the garage. Joan dug too hard and hurt her back, with the result that a month in bed in a nursing home was prescribed. This helped, but she has never fully recovered.

However, keeping to the date on our contract, we posted the finished manuscript to Dents on 31st December 1963. During the next year whilst waiting for proofs, we went on holiday to Madrid from 26th April to 8th May. We stayed in a hotel patronised by Spanish families, some from Guatemala and the Argentine. At dinner (taken far too late for us at 9 or 10 pm) Spanish ladies fanned themselves. We did experience a heatwave. Expeditions were possible to Toledo, Segovia and Avila. In Madrid we haunted the Prado, and bought many slides which we still show in lectures. Best of all the heat benefitted Joan's back.

Getting to know Yorkshire was published at 15s on 3rd September 1964. (In the meantime *The Yorkshire Dales* was being planned for an Aldine paperback.) Reviews, usually short and sometimes in with those of other books, were good. The *Yorkshire Post* stated that 'From the standpoint of accuracy these two Wensleydale writers can be congratulated. ... *Getting to know Yorkshire* is an achievement in condensation'. *The Northern Echo* pleased us by offering the book as a prize for teenagers in a 'Write a Review' competition. Somehow emphasis on the book's status as a children's book failed. Instead of a view which Marie drew for the book wrapper, she should have pictured children. It was an attractive little book, which sold reasonably well, but never found a niche.

LIFE AND TRADITION IN THE YORKSHIRE DALES

When in 1965 we proposed to write a book on what we thought of as 'Customs' in the Dales, we knew that it was an important decision, which might take a long time to bear fruit, and therefore if it did not work out, it would waste precious time. It was plain that a revolution was transforming the old order in most facets of Dales' life. The craftsmen's products had been taken over by mass production, the agricultural depression of the 1930s had reduced the number of holdings, of which many were too small to be viable. The Second World War saw the switch from horses to tractors for motive power, with the introduction of costly new machinery. Farmhouse cheese-making had almost ceased. Also the arrival of electricity had a dramatic effect on both house and farm. All this, the old ways of life rapidly disappearing, needed recording.

We wondered whether we should find any horses working on the farms, any craftsmen exercising their skills, any cast-iron fireplaces with 'reckons' (which had been left in wills in the Middle Ages). As it turned out, we were surprised at what we did find — five farms still using horses, a number of cast-iron and other old ranges, a few farmers cutting peat for fuel, a few women making cheese, quilts and rugs, one baking riddlebread (oatcake), a blacksmith here and there, several shoemakers, one or two cloggers and sadlers, joiners and masons in abundance, and tools lying unused in workshops for thirty years or more, ready to be brought out to make backcans or cart wheels. In 1965 many old practices had gone, but there were people still living who remembered and could demonstrate them. Not so very long after we had finished our research, many of these folk had retired or died. We were literally just in the nick of time.

Our last three books had involved journeying all over Yorkshire, and in the case of *Yorkshire Portraits* all over England, so that it was a relief to be able to work from home. On 7th January, 1965, a diary entry reads: 'Photographs arrived from Sinclair. Sorted them out for illustrating articles. Wrote a list for customs book.' On 1st February we sent a synopsis to Bozzie at Dents for an illustrated book to be called 'Country Life in the Yorkshire Dales'. After discussion with colleagues, he approved the idea.

Obviously photography was to become an important tool in our equipment. The reference to Sinclair was to a firm then based in Whitehall, London, where our films were processed and enlargements made. (For our work they had followed on from E H Horner, photographer, of Settle, a personal friend, who had died.) They also specialised in copying old photographs, and, realising their value, usually sent a postcard acknowledging receipt. Occasionally we suffered agonies of anxiety if delays occurred in the post. Looking back now, we must have borrowed hundreds of old photographs, had them copied, and returned them to their owners. In all these transactions we only misplaced two, both of which eventually turned up.

Marie had a Rolleiflex camera with a lens of proven quality, with which to take the

Cricket Hill, where we stayed with Anne Schlabach on the campus of Bennington College, Vermont.

black-and-white photographs then usual for book production. It took square prints, 2¼ by 2¼ inches, which conveniently allowed four prints on a page to show the stages of craftsmen's work. But, unlike modern cameras, it had neither self-focusing nor self-timing, nor wide-angle nor telephoto lens. For exposures, small bulbs were fixed in a flash gun , and the camera screwed on a tripod, in our case an old simple one. We remember, once in a blacksmith's shop, tripod and camera keeled over on to the ground. Damage resulted and repairs were necessary. For all these drawbacks Marie considers that most of her best photographs were taken with the Rolleiflex.

It is surprising to remember how many holidays and interests we enjoyed during the three years of work on the book. In the spring of 1965 we joined a Swan Hellenic cruise to Greece and Turkey, and in addition to a packed programme to famous sites, we sat at the same table for meals with an American, Anne Schlabach, and became friends. That same year, in the autumn we went on a National Trust tour to Russia, to Moscow and Leningrad, a never-to-be-forgotten experience seeing the wonderful palaces, the Hermitage, the Bolshoi Ballet and much besides.

The Ukraine, our hotel in Moscow in 1965.

Then in the following year, 1966, we went on our own to America, visiting New York, Washington and Williamsburg, and staying with Anne Schlabach in Vermont at the time of the 'fall', when the countryside blazed with colour. Anne was on the philosophy faculty at Bennington College, and later she married Fred Burkhardt, former president of Bennington. Then Fred undertook a huge project to publish all the letters of Charles Darwin, which brought them annually to Cambridge, and so made possible short annual holidays with us here in the Dales and elsewhere. It has been and still is a very happy and long lasting friendship.

On the home front, in 1965 regular contributions were still being made to the 'Country and Coast' feature of the *Yorkshire Post*. In the same year Marie was chairman of the Askrigg Parish Council, and besides routine business had to grapple with the Commons Registration Act. Meetings of the Askrigg Art Club were an ongoing responsibility, and also that year the Askrigg Women's Institute entered a nationwide competition for a village scrapbook. It became a major enterprise enthusiastically taken up by a committee in which we took a leading role. We won first prize for the Yorkshire region, but failed to win at national level. (Secretly we all thought our scrapbook superior to the winner.) No wonder 'very tired' sometimes turns up in the diaries.

All this must have hindered but did not deter. We soon planned to add to the text and photographs, pages of drawings depicting the specialised equipment of farm and house, much of it no longer in use. At length we were driven to buying the bulk of the bygones in order to make drawings of them. So we scanned the advertisements in local papers of sales all over the Dales, and rushed off to likely venues. Whilst on the whole these items sold for very little, the forays were time-consuming. At a sale at Romaldkirk in Teesdale we waited from 12 noon to about 6 o'clock in order to buy a Mark Metcalfe grandfather clock (for £24), and carried it home sticking out of the boot of the car. Bygones were often thrown in with desirable modern things, and the buyer would usually gladly part with these for a matter of shillings, thus getting what he wanted for nothing and pleasing us.

Besides all this, several people gave us treasures. Our longstanding friends from Stone House, upper Swaledale, moved from their outlying farm and offered us many rare farm and household paraphenalia, including a bacon flake, a rack on which bacon and hams were laid to dry. (We actually photographed this *in situ*.) Our acquisitions, stored in an outhouse, eventually formed the basis of the Dales Countryside Museum at Hawes.

In addition we checked up on farming and domestic matters in other parts of the country, and both wrote to curators and visited their folk museums There were the Museum of English Rural Life at Reading with a battery of card indices to be consulted, the National Museum of Antiquities at Edinburgh with interesting displays, the Castle Museum at York relevant to our research, and the Bowes Museum at Barnard Castle with a local section. Perhaps for a museum of local life the Welsh Folk Museum at St Fagans Castle, Cardiff, was outstanding. Here we were allowed to take photographs, had records in Welsh translated for us, and made friends with the then curator, Fransis Payne.

Our field-work bore rewarding results, and the following pages record some of the highlights. One of the first photographs we took was of our neighbour making a hooky rug in the farmhouse kitchen, with a then typical background of a ham, rolls of bacon, shoes on a ceiling shelf and a grandfather clock. Seeking out old kitchen ranges became something of an obsession, and led to entry into farmhouses and other discoveries such as cupboard beds. The owners themselves and sometimes a cat added to the scene, as at Agglethorpe Hall, where a black range had been fitted into the alcove of a seventeenth-century arch. At Blayshaw in upper Nidderdale we found a perfect example of a fireplace cast at the Todd foundry in that dale, and at West Nettlepot, Baldersdale, we were entertained by one of our hosts playing an accordion sitting by the fireplace. These often elderly people welcomed us, and we responded warmly to such genuine unspoilt folk. At Blayshaw they lent us photographs of sheep-washing once undertaken before clipping, with the crowds that used to assemble on these occasions as if for an entertainment. We more than once returned to Nettlepot, but some years later, visiting Blayshaw, we were told that our friends had died.

Next to these kitchens there were the whitewashed dairies with tiers of stone shelves containing plates of food, milk cans, colandars, bowls, tins, churns, butter hands and pails. We remember Mrs Mason of Ingman Lodge, upper Ribblesdale, describing butter-making as a knack needing 'a light hand like pastry-making'. Another time we visited Black Howe, upper Swaledale, where one of the daughters, Eleanor, took us through the stages of butter-making. Like Mrs Mason, she emphasised the need for scrupulous cleanliness, scalding implements, and frequently washing hands and rubbing them with oatmeal. Here, too, at Black Howe we attended a quilt-making session that entailed quilting frames and traditional patterns handed down in the family. Formerly daughters made a quilt in anticipation of marriage.

Luck is inevitably an ingredient in work such as ours. Always taking the camera with us, by chance we passed a group of men clipping sheep on the summit of the Buttertubs Pass, a farmer from Muker walling a gap, and another near Keld jagging hay. We had thought that jagging had gone out with packhorses. Swaledale offered splendid backgrounds for such scenes. Another day, arriving at the bridge over the Ribble at Horton-in-Ribblesdale, we had a hunch that we should turn up the side road to New Houses. There we met two brothers, John and Richard Wallbank, who, becoming interested in our project, offered to salve a sheep, a long-abandoned autumn practice. A day was arranged and photographs taken. They told us later that the sheep had thrived on its old-fashioned treatment. They also gave us an introduction to a cousin, William Wallbank of Keasden near Settle. William told us of huge gatherings of men on clipping days, and said 'It's all work now, now that the crafts have gone.' He meant that work and pleasure have become separated, whereas in the past to join in communal activities such as sheep clipping or washing was in itself a pleasure. It was a trenchant comment, and a glimpse of a past mores, 'of the world we have lost'. In turn he told us of a Miss Elsie Carr at a farm nearby, who had only recently ceased to make riddlebread (if we remember rightly because her uncle had loved it).

Dentdale.

The subject of oatcake appealed to us, and we tracked down the many regional varieties found from Wharfedale and Ribblesdale to Swaledale. Arranging a day, we went to the farmhouse near Bentham, where Elsie Carr prepared batter and baked riddlebread on a heated bakestone with skill and dexterity. It was a rare occasion, possibly the most traditional happening that we witnessed. We remember that it snowed as we returned up Ribblesdale, and reached home safely feeling elated. Recently a friend had the ingredients of oatcake analysed, and found that it gave instant energy, the equivalent of a glass of whisky.

We were recommended to visit a farmhouse at Gawthrop, Dent, where we found a disused back kitchen. It contained a cast-iron fireplaces with an adjoining backstone, a slopstone (stone sink), and a large stone cheese-press. But the fireplace and bakestone were obscured by a large heap of coke, so with permission we shovelled it away, a dusty business, in order to take a photograph. Another day we were directed by a friend, Teddy Dinsdale, to visit a farmhouse near Sedbergh, where we found in the kitchen an old range and alongside it a bakestone papered over. As all this was about to be replaced by a new fireplace, we settled to buy the bakestone for one pound. But when we went to arrange transport to Askrigg, we found the iron plate cracked right across. We hesitated whether to take it, to the consternation of the farmer's wife, who feared the loss of her pound. However we stuck to our bargain, and the bakestone is installed in the Dales Countryside Museum with the crack filled in.

For farming it was necessary to follow the round of the seasons. A pair of creels, a rope and hazel bow contraption, was used to carry hay to the sheep in winter, and we photographed Jim Alderson of Keld using a pair out on the pastures. William Hunter,

Swaledale sheep waiting to be fed: (above) winter on Malham Moor; (below) at Ribblehead, March 1989, against a background of the railway viaduct and Whernside.

of Crow Trees near Muker, we saw mucking with a horse and coup cart, and he later made us a pair of creels, and showed us the age-old method of making a burden of hay which prevailed before balers were introduced. Our good friends, the Porters, invited us to attend a sheep-clipping at High Oxnop, an old farmhouse in the Oxnop valley, and we joined them for elevenses and took photographs.

Haytime with sweeps and sledges pulled by horses found us taking photographs in Grisedale, Garsdale and Swaledale. At Moor Close farm near Thwaite we chanced to see Cherry Kearton sweeping hay to a barn, as black clouds heralding a thunderstorm loomed not far away. We took photographs as best we could, then turned to and helped, one of us in the mew, and the camera laid down in the grass. Photographs taken on this farm against a background of Great Shunnor Fell are spectacular. One of the thunderstorm photographs made a fine subject for the book jacket.

At the head of Baldersdale we made friends with the Icetons of Blackton, where we saw them using a wing sweep pulled by a horse. Sweeps, wooden implements for haymaking, varied in different dales, developed to suit the lie of the land. Similarly we found that every dale had a different pattern of peat spade, a tool of great age, with a small wing so that it cut a short and a long side to make a peat.

In October 1965 we were directed to Low Birk Hatt, a farm adjoining the Icetons, where we were told there lived someone who was old-fashioned and possessed old-fashioned things. The old-fashioned lady was Hannah Hauxwell, then aged thirty-nine, who eight years later was to become famous. She invited us in and showed us many treasures, from four-poster beds to top hats, filling the main sitting-room and the bedrooms. Later we sent her a Christmas card. We saw Hannah again the following year, and asked if we could take a photograph of her with a stand churn bound with ash bands, but she demurred and, respecting her privacy, we did not persist. Others later were more persuasive! At the time we did not know her dire financial circumstances, but, thinking of our collection, we offered to buy the churn. However she graciously preferred to loan it. It is still on loan at the Dales Countryside Museum in Hawes.

Besides farming there were the craftsmen. Frank Shields of Redmire made us a metal backcan for carrying milk using his tinsmith equipment, whilst we made a photographic record. William Thompson of Hawes made us a cart wheel using his wheelwright tools, which he later donated to us. These men had not practiced their craft for years, but never hesitated for a minute. At Barbon near Sedbergh the Tallons, blacksmiths, were able to hoop a cart wheel, because from time to time gipsies on their way to the Westmorland fairs brought the wheel of a caravan to hoop.

From all this time we do not remember a single rebuff, instead a genuine welcome. Perhaps we brought a diversion to some who led uneventful lives. These stalwart Dalespeople enjoyed talking about old times, and appreciated having them recorded. Many thanked us for the photographs which we sent as a token of their co-operation.

In May 1968, Marie was awarded an Honorary MA by Leeds University for the books already published, particularly *Yorkshire Village,* but as the honours list for that year was full, Joan was promised an honour later (which did not materialise). For Marie the ceremony was daunting, but she appreciated the address given by Professor Maurice Beresferd and a talk on the Dales with Sir Roger Stephens, the vice-chancellor. In July we sent off the manuscript, drawings and photographs to Dents. Over the last three years we had kept up a correspondence with them, and had visited London for discussions. We were warned that the book was going to be expensive, as production costs were constantly rising.

In August 1965, Bozzie had retired as editor at Dents. Alas, sadly word came through in June 1967 that he had fallen seriously ill and had died. Bozzie was a scholar with wide interests. He had written one or two novels, and had edited Dents current encyclopedia. He had also been a mountaineer, and a member of the Alpine Club. For us he had been a good friend, guiding us in our work for thirty years. Such continuity is a pearl without price. It was a drastic break, and relations with Dents were never quite the same again.

We then began with a new man, Michael Geare, who enthusiastically steered the book through to publication. It was his idea to have such a lot of photographs, and he wrote that he thought it would prove to be 'a handsome, unique, and authoritative piece of work'. We had already signed a contract in February 1967 which stipulated completion by the end of the year — a clause we failed to implement — and also ninety pages of photographs, which worked out at about 260 in total. Of these, 200 were ours, taken mostly during the last three years. Up to the end the title posed problems. 'Traditional Dales Life', which had replaced the first version, proved unacceptable to the publicity staff. On 4th April 1968, Michael Geare wrote, 'I think we must finally climb out of our respective baths and settle for the title *Life and Tradition in the Yorkshire Dales*'. Eventually this was copied and used by others, as if it were the most obvious in the world, whereas it had been arrived at after hours of anxious thought.

When the book was published in September 1968 it cost £4 4s, then regarded as a high price. Reviews in both local and national papers were long and favourable. The book was discussed at length in the radio programme *The World of Books*, chaired by Ronald Eyre. Pat Williams approved of 'the kind of loving way the subject is treated,' and Janet Adam Smith praised the marvellous collection of photographs. Even Arthur Raistrick in the *Yorkshire Post* wrote: 'On rare occasions a book appears which will become a standard reference book for many generations.'

Dents were delighted with pre-publication sales, and raised our royalties. Later one person criticised us for not including religion, nor for that matter did we tackle dialect, but a book can be overburdened with subjects, and these do not come under the heading of folk life. We presumably attended signing sessions at bookshops, but records fail us here. In October we were invited as guest authors at a Yorkshire Post Literary Luncheon at the Queen's Hotel, Leeds, the first of a few appearances at these prestigous functions.

About this time someone from ITV knocked at our door, and thanked us for giving them the idea of a *Farmhouse Kitchen* programme, one that lasted for years. Less welcome were other ITV people who sought out Dalesfolk featured in the book to interview them for television. Some responded and some did not. Ideas are not copyright!

What pleased us was meeting members with similar interests at a conference of the Society of Folk Life Studies at Bangor University in August 1960. A member, George Ewart Evans, well-known for his work and publications on traditional life, had been sent a review copy of our book. He introduced us to other members, including Dr Iowerth Peate, a pioneer in folk-life studies and a former keeper of the Welsh Folk Museum. In our research we had ploughed a lonely furrow, so it was an exceptionally heart-warming experience to meet and talk to such distinguished scholars working in the same field.

LIFE AND TRADITION IN THE MOORLANDS OF NORTH-EAST YORKSHIRE

As *Life and Tradition in the Yorkshire Dales* had proved to be a success, we began to consider another area suitable for a book to be approached in the same way. We had not far to look. Across the Vale of York were the moorlands of North-East Yorkshire, a compact region of a similar size to the Dales, and similarly designated as a National Park. What is more we knew it quite well, but only as visitors. First it was necessary to discover whether some of the leading authorities on folk life over there would feel us to be an intrusion or would welcome us.

One day in January 1969 we motored over to the moorlands, and sought out Bert Frank, curator of the Ryedale Folk Museum, at Hutton-le-Hole. We enquired whether he wished to write such a book, and he replied that he did not. But he thought it an excellent idea, and would help us all he could. Bert and his wife, Evelyn, who lived in a house adjoining the museum at Hutton-le-Hole, eventually became firm friends, and as Evelyn took in guests, we often stayed there as a base for work. Bert Frank, then aged fifty-six, was born at Hutton. Briefly he started life as a farm man, graduated to be a farmer, became interested in bygone tools and implements, and when in 1963 the Misses Crosland, members of a Quaker family, offered him three rooms in their house at Hutton, he opened a museum. Meanwhile Evelyn helped the Croslands, and when they died, Bert was left the property, where he and his wife were living on the occasion of our visit. Bert was a man with a vision, year by year adding to the objects which became the Ryedale Folk Museum. In course of time the long grassy croft behind the house provided sites for several ancient buildings brought beam by beam and stone by stone from nearby places. He was the inspiration for a team of voluntary workers who gradually built up the different displays with their own hands. We never failed to admire his dedication

Bert Frank with a corn dolly that he has made, c1970.

and constant hard work. In 1970 whilst we were staying there, the manor house from Harome, a village a few miles away, was dismantled and re-erected in the croft — a major task, first entailing rearing three huge pairs of crucks.

Raymond Hayes, photographer and archeologist.

Although we did not meet him on that January day, we were introduced later to Raymond Hayes, who lived at Hutton, who was a photographer and archaeologist. His father, William Hayes (1871-1940), was a York photographer who moved to Hutton in the 1920s. Thus through Raymond we were offered the choice of a large collection of his father's and his own photographs. Many were and are period pieces with the special flavour of the 1920s. It is worth saying that later both Raymond and Bert have been awarded the MBE. How fortunate we were to find these two generous men, with whom incidentally we have not lost touch to this day.

On the same day in January 1969 we crossed the moors to the Esk Valley, and branched off to Westerdale to Low House where the Fairfax-Blakeboroughs lived. At that time Major Fairfax-Blakeborough, then aged eighty-six, was writing for local papers a syndicated column, which, because of his lifetime's knowledge of rural subjects, was always full of interest. We were invited into his study lined with books, and met his wife. We again asked if we should be trespassing on his territory if we wrote a book on folk life in the moorlands, and like Bert he welcomed our project and offered his help. It was the start of a warm relationship with him and his wife, who invariably gave us a cup of tea whenever we called. He was the son of Richard Blakeborough, who throughout his life had collected folk tales, and was the author of a classic, *Yorkshire, Wit, Character, Folk Lore and Customs* (1898). The major explains in the preface to one of his books *The Hand of Glory* (1924) that he inherited from his father a mass of material comprising old songs, quaint stories, traditional folk tales, curious beliefs and customs, and he himself had a lifetime's work behind him of 100 or more books and publications on horses, racing and country life. He wrote *The Cleveland Bay*, and later introduced us to well-known breeders. We remember the major taking a book out of a bookcase to find us a reference, blowing the dust off it, and stuffing back newspaper cuttings and other papers stored in its pages. On 10th March

Major and Mrs J Fairfax-Blakeborough at Low House, Westerdale, c1971.

Seth Eccles thatching the Manor House in 1971, moved from Harome to the Ryedale Folk Museum.

1969 he wrote in a letter 'We loved your visit. We look forward to your next visit ... and send hearts' warmth and friendship plus admiration for your work.' Some years later he was given the OBE, and he died aged ninety-two in 1976.

During the next two years Bert Frank, Raymond Hayes, and the major and several other friends gave us introductions to neighbours and people they thought might help. Nothing could have been of more value, especially as we were away from home, and time was precious. These informants must have saved us hours of time, and probably made the book possible. Of course we had chance encounters as we had had in the Dales, and we often branched out on our own initiative.

We were all set to go, except that we had to make arrangements to stay in the moorlands. There, too, fortune favoured us. As we have said, we stayed with the Franks at Hutton, on the spot for the Ryedale Folk Museum. At Kirkbymoorside we were taken in by Mr and Mrs J W Underwood, whose house became a home from home. Mr Underwood was a postman, and so went to bed early and rose early. Joan, whose job it was to write up the day's notes, was often last up, and locked the house up each night. Mrs Underwood's family had been bakers, and so we learnt about food such as frumety and gingerbread. We were always given a box of fruit and vegetables from their large garden to take home with us at the weekend, and they still visit us. On the other side of our territory we stayed in Glaisdale at Postgate Farm with the Thompson family, and again benefitted from their friendly co-operation. Their house had a witch post, in the buildings was a barn thresher, and in the fields a cider press. We stayed once with the Sleightholmes at Goathland, where Mr

Sleightholme and his fore-elders had been joiners, and recollected funeral customs. Charges ranged from 30s to £2 each a day full board with packed lunch. Present-day prices would have been prohibitive for us. We never sought grants from public funds, and indeed should very likely not have been given any. As it was we were very fortunate in our rooms.

Joan Ingilby, president of the Askrigg Produce Show, with Mrs M E Hooper, former president, in 1974

Most weeks from Monday to Friday from April to October, we motored across the Vale of York, and each weekend at home tended our large garden, fed the hens which had been looked after whilst we were away, and made ready for the next week. During these years in 1970 Joan had been elected president of the Askrigg Produce Association Show, held in late August or early September. It had been started in the war in the Dig for Victory campaign,

Hanging pictures at the 1979 Askrigg Produce Show: Joan Ingilby, Professor T B Worth, Marie Hartley and Mr Collins.

and as gardeners we had always supported it by membership of the committee. The show also had an art section, which we enjoyed hanging. But recently it had lost impetus, and entries to classes had fallen drastically, so Joan spent time urging everyone who could to enter. She had help from Margaret Hopper who, together with her husband, former presidents, had kept the event on a professional level. This resulted in a new start with full tables of exhibits. In 1995 the show goes on as one of the most enjoyable days in the village calendar.

In the second year our American friend, Anne Schlabach from Bennington College, Vermont, came to stay with us at Kirkbymoorside. She fell for the beauty of the moorlands, especially Farndale, also our favourite dale, and she was surprised at the lifestyle of a postman's family, who had a huge croft-garden and four greenhouses.

During the next two years we were constantly made aware of the difference between the Dales and the moorlands. On either side of the high moors small dales slope down, Farndale, Rosedale, and Bilsdale on the south towards the Vale of Pickering, and Glaisdale, Fryup, Danbydale and Westerdale northwards into the Esk valley. A host of new features in house, farm, people and customs confronted and delighted us. In an article on 'Evolution of Yorkshire Dalesfolk' in an early number of the *Dalesman*, Fairfax-Blakeborough wrote: 'Environment indubitably has a tremendous effect upon mentality as well as upon physique on life itself as well as upon outlook and attitude to life'.

It was not until November 1969 that Dents commissioned the book. Michael Geare had left, and one or two new editors, whom we never met, followed. They specified that the book should be on the same lines as before, that is with drawings, tools and implements, and 260 photographs. This time there was no need to buy anything. It was all there in the Ryedale Folk Museum, Beck Isle and Whitby museums, or in waggon sheds and craftsmen's workshops.

Also a large collection of old photographs lay at hand, taken by professional photographers living in the area. At Whitby, Frank Meadow Sutcliffe (1853-1941) was nationally renowned, best known for his Whitby scenes, but penetrating inland with his camera, often to Lealholm in the Esk Valley. We were delighted with two Sutcliffe photographs of sheep washing on the moors. But their whereabouts were unknown, and we spent a day, like detectives, tracking them down from place to place and farm to farm. We bought seventeen Sutcliffe prints for £29.75 at the Eglon Shaw gallery in Whitby. Once after we had left our camera behind at home, Eglon Shaw lent us one.

At the Whitby Museum the librarian of the Whitby Literary and Philosophical Society, Percy Burnett, took immense trouble to find the glass plates of Thomas Watson of Lythe (1863-1957). A few photographs of T Page of Rosedale had survived, including a famous one of ten men and boys scything corn and tying sheaves by hand prior to the introduction of reapers. (Rumour had it that the glass plates had been used to build a greenhouse.) Other early photographs were taken at Goathland by Oxley Grabham, c1910, curator of the Yorkshire Museum at York. At Pickering, Sydney Smith (1884-1958), had caught many atmospheric scenes, and his wife, who was living in the town, lent us nine prints which we had copied. When we returned them, she surprised us by giving us a box of chocolates. We used ten modern photographs of J Tindale of Whitby, and others lent us single prints to copy. No doubt the proliferation of photographers in north-east Yorkshire arose from its photogenic coastal scenes and the numbers of visitors who came here in early days. They can be matched by the artists such as Dame Laura Knight who settled for a time at Staithes. In the end, out of 265 plates in the book only 147 were ours. A few of these were treasures — a set of thatching photographs taken in Farndale when Ella Pontefract and Marie were writing *Yorkshire Tour*, and another which appears to be unique of a horse-wheel with man and horse in action.

Nonetheless we took hundreds of photographs. As before we first concentrated on fireside scenes, prints of which sent to the people concerned pleased them, as many letters testify. These cast-iron ranges had been cast at local foundries. We were advised to see J W Carter of the Cyclops Foundry at Kirkbymoorside, then elderly and rather frail, and so recorded recollections that would have been lost. A feature of the fireplaces was the hearth plate designed for the burning of peat or turf, and in addition there were special cast-iron pans, such as the *yetling*, which could serve as an oven. Some of these utensils were used for baking turf cakes, a kind of scone, and a local speciality.

A few families, including the Thompsons, still cut peat in the deep bogs of the moorland heights, but formerly droves of people once set out for the day on such forays. Over near Goathland, turf was cut from the surface of the moor with huge spades. We took photographs of the Smailes and the Grahams of Hunt House cutting turves, and of turf stacks drying against a background of the 'golf balls' of the Fylingdales Early Warning Station. The heather moors were ever-present: for sheep strays, for peat and turf, for *eldin* (kindling), for thatching, for besoms, for nectar for bees, for bog myrtle for a drink, and for bilberries for pies.

The antiquity of the region struck us: the medieval crosses, the pannier ways, the ancient construction of many houses, with crucks, cross passages, witch posts, box beds, salt boxes and thatched roofs. We visited several: Spout House and Carr Cote in Bilsdale, Duck House and Oak Crag in Farndale, the last alas burnt down some years later, and made drawings or took photographs. At Goathland ling (heather) has been used for thatching, and the lovely watercolours of Mary Weatherill portrayed humble cottages huddled like bundles of heather on the moorland landscape.

We tracked down all the remaining witch posts, including two at the Pitt Rivers Museum at Oxford, and found that they were not known in Ireland or Scotland. A hundred years ago, belief in witches prevailed, and stories of their power, spells, shapeshifting and persecution have been preserved by Richard Blakeborough and by Canon Atkinson in his classic book *Forty Years in a Moorland Parish*, published first in 1891. In Goathland a few such stories of witches still lingered on, passed down by word of mouth. Formerly, too, hobs and fairies abounded, the former sometimes malevolent and sometimes mischievous. Such folklore without doubt had existed in other parts of Yorkshire, but here superstitious beliefs persisted in the fastnesses of remote dales, and some were fortunately recorded.

Marie and Joan in their vegetable garden.

Joan feeding the hens, which we kept up to the bad winter of 1979.

The most obvious difference between the western dales and the moorlands was in the type of farming, partially pastoral, but combined with the cultivation of arable land, especially along the borders with the Vale of Pickering. We well remember Bert Frank explaining to us the intricacies of the rotation of crops, and the actual practice of ploughing with two horses, which we found complicated. In addition there was sowing, harvesting, stacking and threshing. We were told of the first put-off reapers superseded by self-binders, of flails and threshing sets with steam engines, and barn threshers driven by horse-wheels, occasionally water wheels, and one by a pony paddling.

We chanced upon a farmer sowing small seeds by hand on a farm in Bilsdale, and as an added bonus he mustered a neighbour, and they posed playing merrills, a game of great age, on a corn bin lid. Similarly we were told to go to Raw Farm near Robin Hood's Bay to see butter-making, and in addition found the farmer sowing corn, later lazybanding to sow turnip seed, and still more the farmhouse 107 feet long, in effect a longhouse. It has to be said that, on other occasions, following up suggestions sometimes proved disappointing.

One day motoring up Farndale we noticed a farmer opening out a field of oats preparatory to harvesting it, and asked permission to take photographs. Two families on two farms were involved, and as a son drove a tractor pulling a self-binder, the womenfolk made stooks in the old style. One of these photographs was used eventually for the book jacket. Later we also attended a threshing day on one of these same farms. What nice people they were! Threshing days occurring in the autumn were well remembered, busy scenes that attracted the early photographers. In our book

Harvesting in Farndale.

we arranged two adjoining plates, one showing thirteen men at a threshing day in 1948, and the other in 1970 with just two men sitting on two combine harvesters, which did away with self-binders, threshing sets and threshing days.

We met many craftsmen at the May Day celebrations at the Ryedale Folk Museum — for example Arthur Robinson, miller at Rievaulx, and Frank Wetherill, mason from Eskdale — and followed up these introductions. One day, with the scene organised by Bert Frank, we took a photograph of a saw pit at the head of Farndale, with Bert's son and a neighbouring farmer acting as top and bottom sawyer. Another day in August we set off to the moors to take photographs of the many hives of bees out there for nectar from the heather flowers. We hid behind a wall, but never dare raise our heads for the bees whizzing over it on the way to their hives. But several beekeepers told us fascinating bee lore. Others remembered the former harvest of fruit grown in orchards along the edge of the Vale of Pickering, so important that formerly tons of gooseberries, and stones of plums and apples were picked to be sold at markets, to shops and to jam factories. What a pity this has gone, as orchards were neglected in wars, and foreign fruit was imported.

The community spirit of former days was everywhere evident. Pride in work held people together. Following flittings (removals), neighbours offered a horse and plough for a ploughing day. Once there were cruck-rearing, sheep-clipping, pig-killing and bee-taking days. It used to be said in Farndale that 'if one was poorly they were all poorly'. Life could be harsh. 'You had to earn your bread where you could.' Hirings for farm and domestic servants had long gone, but were remembered.

During those years we worked hard, but, looking back, they seem like a holiday, with brilliant sunshine and never a day's rain. Sometimes we returned to our rooms on the moorland road from Castleton to Hutton in a state of euphoria after a succesful day's work. It cannot be said that our fieldwork had been in the nick of time. We occasionally met people who bemoaned that someone had died who had had a good memory. But we did benefit from whole-hearted support and graphic recollections.

We posted off the manuscript and illustrations just before Christmas 1971. Production for an illustrated book took many months and involved many letters. Again the title was discussed and agreed on. At this time an American edition of *Life and Tradition in the Yorkshire Dales* came out, partly as a result of meeting publishers on our visit to America and Canada. Dents actually had an office in Toronto where we stayed a weekend with friends. Called *Vanishing Folkways*, it was not a success — too close to modern times. Dents were disappointed that the book on the moorlands was not chosen for a prize by the *Yorkshire Post*. At this time they were considering launching a series using our Dale book as a prototype for different regions of England. Five were eventually brought out on the Lake District, Northumberland and Durham, Suffolk and North-East Essex, the Cotswolds, and Rural Wales. Some, written by well-known folklife scholars, were good, but others less so. No doubt it was difficult to find the right people with time to spare for research.

In November 1972 the book was published in the same format as the Dales book, but at £5.75 instead of £4 4s, showing the inexorable rise in costs and prices. Dents were pleased with sales and reception. John Whitney, deputy literary editor of *The Sunday Times,* reviewed it from personal knowledge of the area. Major Fairfax-Blakeborough wrote: 'If the YP had sent it to me to review, I should in all truth have given it praise as a Yorkshire classic.' We had met and visited Dr Brenda Riddells at Sleights, who herself wrote novels, and whose father was Dr Thomas English, the compiler of two handsome volumes *Whitby Prints.* She wrote: 'Your moorlands is certainly the most outstanding work on the area to be brought out in my lifetime.' Finally Martin Dent chose the book as his favourite publication that year for a series on publisher's choice in *Time and Tide.*

LIFE AND TRADITION IN WEST YORKSHIRE

A third book in the 'Life and Tradition' series seemed feasible. At first we thought of the Wolds of the East Riding, where a farmer friend expressed interest, and indeed he and his wife put us up for a night with the intention of introducing us to the region. Such a book would have been well worthwhile, but it seemed to us too similar to the moorlands from the farming angle. All the processes of corn-growing would be repeated. Also it is a small area, not quite viable from a publisher's point of view. Reluctantly we gave it up, and had to disappoint our friends.

Instead we turned to the Industrial West Riding, then after boundary changes divided into West Yorkshire and South Yorkshire. West Yorkshire covered a compact area, with the towns of Huddersfield and Halifax and villages in the Pennines on the west, and the cities of Leeds and Bradford and many towns and villages on the east. To include South Yorkshire would have brought in another culture altogether, and to do justice to both would, we thought, have made too long a book. So West Yorkshire alone was chosen.

The scenario could not have been more different from the dales and moorlands: conurbations with busy town centres, imposing public buildings, huge Nonconformist chapels, great mills and factories, bristling chimneys, stretches of open country, endless streets lined with terraced houses, and Pennine valleys invaded by industry but with heather moors. A scene of great endeavour set in a landscape of dark millstone grit.

There were advantages in our choice. Both of us were born in the West Riding — Joan at North Stainley, near Ripon, on the edge of open countryside, and Marie at Morley, a town near Leeds, thoroughly industrialised. Marie's connections and childhood recollections were of value in themselves, and her family's occupation as manufacturers in the textile industry, one which dominated the region, would obviously be of importance in our work.

Also Marie's sister-in-law, Rosalie Hartley, had lived in Leeds all her life. Because of the death of her husband, Marie's brother, we had become close, and, entering into the spirit of the project, she offered hospitality, which we enjoyed for many weeks in her large family home. She introduced us to heads of firms in a city of a multitude of large and small businesses — wholesale clothing, forges, engineers, makers of railway rolling stock, wire, cap, sauce and relish makers, crockery shops and department stores, so many in fact that it was hard to do justice to them all. Also the environs of Leeds and Bradford, the Spen Valley and Airedale were within range. But for this support, especially the hospitality, the book might never have got off the ground.

As well, a cousin of Marie's, John Hartley, had married Eva Crowther, a daughter of one of the manufacturers of that name in the Colne Valley, which branched off from Huddersfield, and they too put us up. Her father, Guy Crowther of Crimble

Mills, Slaithwaite, guided us through the intricacies of the textile industry, arranged meetings with his retired workpeople, and introduced us to a relative, a widow, Peggy Crowther, who also offered us hospitality in a large Victorian house in the valley. When her husband died, she had taken on the chairmanship of the firm, Bank Bottom Mills at Marsden, formerly said to be the largest family-owned mill in the world. She, too, gave us introductions to the staff, and lent us manuscript recollections describing the early years of the last century.

We also stayed at Hebden Bridge at the head of the Calder Valley. Here we had long admired the terraces of double-decker houses massed against the hillside, which had sparked off *The Wonders of Yorkshire*. But we knew little of its trades of corduroy manufacture, ready-made clothing for industrial use, and not far away the clog works which drew our attention.

So, based on these locations, we spent many weeks again from Monday to Friday roughly from May to December in 1973 and 1974. Again we met with ready co-operation. Many people knew our work and had read our books. Directors wished to have the histories and products of their firms recorded, and a host of people related their experiences and life stories.

There were drawbacks. Inevitably we started off in the morning rush hour and returned in the homeward scramble. The complex network of roads meant studying large-scale maps and town plans to guide us to our destinations. One had to be navigator and one driver. Also, instead of dropping in on country folk, here was a region of rigid schedules. Understandably we had to make appointments with heads of firms,

Hebden Bridge.

but also many people were at work, and others on holiday. Then, we soon learnt that townsfolk spoke faster than countryfolk, and within a day or two of starting work, we had to spare time by buy a tape recorder.

Fieldwork meant visiting museums and libraries, of which West Yorkshire is liberally endowed, for information and photographs. Our first contact was at the Leeds Museums, where the curator made helpful suggestions and generously gave us a set of photographs of a clay-pipe maker in a workshop in Leeds. Similarly at the Tolson Memorial Museum at Huddersfield we made friends with the curator, and met an assistant interested in teazles, used in machines for raising the nap of cloth. We later saw teazles growing at Fivehead in Somerset for the Yorkshire trade, a memorable experience. Two new museums were about to open — the Bradford Industrial Museum, and Armley Mills at Leeds. We had a good introduction to the former, for Stuart Feather, the curator, told us that he had read our books at the age of eleven. As before, our aim was predominantly to seek how life was lived in the past by recording personal recollections, thus letting people speak for themselves. We were working at a certain point in time. The dreadful conditions and poverty of the early years of the last century no longer shocked. Slum clearance had gone on apace in the 1920s and onwards, although we heard at first-hand of cellar dwellings and crowded conditions. (Shades of *Mary Barton* by Mrs Gaskell.)

The textile industry, permeating every corner of the region, was to take up a large part of the book. The huge mills were obvious, but in quiet corners, all kinds of ancillary trades were pursued: wire-making, card clothing, bobbin-, shuttle- and picker-making, not to mention the textile machinery makers, from looms to engines to the huge carding machines. The dramatic history of the industry, beginning in the Pennines as the 'domestic system', based on home workshops, and continuing to the throes of the Industrial Revolution, seemed to require a first chapter partially based on printed sources. But to our surprise we met two men in the Colne Valley, and others later, who harked back to hand-loom days, and as a constant reminder of that era, clothiers' houses, such as those at the museum at Golcar, displayed rows of mullion windows (weavers' windows, as they are called).

We talked to both men and women who had worked in the mills; for it has to be remembered that long before women entered the labour market as we know it, they had been essential to the running of a mill as weavers, menders and spinners. At Heptonstall above Hebden Bridge we found Mrs Tupman, whose recollections led back to her father, going to work aged eight, as a doffer at Low Lumb Mill, and in time marrying, bringing up a family, becoming a bandsman and conductor of Heptonstall Band, and dying aged ninety-one. She herself (born in 1882) started work as a half-timer aged ten machining garments. Nowadays we should expect at least damaged health, but here she was, well, with a good memory and happy to talk to us.

At Manningham Mills, Bradford, we were invited to a tea party to meet retired employees, and afterwards we visited some in their homes. (All had curtains of Lister velvet.) One time when we returned to our car at Manningham we found it covered with fine sandy dust as the face of the buildings were being cleaned by sandblasting.

Similarly, the head of Thomas Burnleys at Gomersal Mills introduced us to his retired employees (who were given a gold watch on retirement), and at Salts Mill, Saltaire, when we met workers, they told us that it was regarded as a prestigious mill to get into. At Black Dyke Mills we were taken out to lunch, given the names of men to see, and shown the band room; and at Dean Clough Mills, Halifax, we heard of the 5,000 workforce making carpets, and spoke to a retired boilerman, aged ninety-two, once in charge of eight boilers that burnt eighty tons of coal a day. We were invited to a forget-me-not garden party for the elderly employees of Lockhill Mills, Sowerby Bridge, and were engaged in talk with two former weavers who said how happy they were at work, enjoying the companionship, and finding their way to work on dark mornings by the light of a lighted candle in a jam jar.

Partly through our membership of the Society of Folk Life Studies, and also our previous books, we were offered by the head, Stewart Sanderson, some of the research undertaken by the Institute of Dialect and Folk Life Studies at Leeds University, much of it on gramophone records. This department has unfortunately gone. The *Halifax Courier* became interested, and asked their elderly readers to send in their life stories, which they did.

Very many of these people described how they had begun work in the lowliest job in a mill as a piecer or a doffer on the spinning machines, and had risen, in the case of the men, to be an overlooker or manager. Many had started in the iniquitous system, as we think of it, of half-timers, working half a day and going to school the other half, alternating each week, a system that finished in 1922. We were introduced by a cousin of Marie's, Olive Bedford at Gildersome, near Leeds, to a neighbour who had been a weaver, who gave us her labour certificate dated 5th March 1915, which stated that as she was now thirteen, and had made 350 attendances at school during the last five years, she could start work, which she did, as a piecer. She left when she married, and she was one of the few who had not enjoyed the mill. Most had taken a pride in their work, and had revelled in the companionship. Many, both men and women, had worked for the same firm for over fifty years. A local historian at Morley spoke of the 'ladies of the mill' who would do anything for you.

In actual fact, labour relations were good in the textile industry. We met the first woman to be president of a chamber of commerce in England, who said that, in the old days, everyone was happy if they had a good employer, and she felt strongly that 'the whole country depends on what the workers produce'. We also began to hear the distant knell of this great historic Yorkshire trade. The head of a firm making textile machinery, wrote in a letter: 'I get very depressed sometimes at the present state of our textile industry with the resultant closures which are taking place at the moment there seems to end to it'.

Another industry, coal, had almost left West Yorkshire, as the deeper seams of South Yorkshire were exploited. Nonetheless we found a few elderly miners able to give us a picture of the work as it once was. One man, Syd Thompson of Rothwell in particular, took infinite trouble to tell us his life story. He started in a Durham mine at the age of fourteen, earning 11s a week as a pony driver, and by self-education

The heights of the Calder Valley, seen from near Warley.

In the valley bottom is Dean Clough Mills, Halifax, photographed in 1974. Once the Crossley carpet factory, employing some 5,000 people, it closed in 1982, and now houses 160 companies.

Brodsworth Colliery.

ended up as a manager of Rothwell Collieries. Another man, aged ninety-seven, remembered the Featherstone Riots in 1903, notorious because soldiers were called out. The coal industry, so different from textiles, has a tragic history of strikes, lock-outs, and disastrous accidents resulting in many deaths. Yet again those we spoke to had taken pride in their work, and had enjoyed the comradeship. In 1974 mining had become totally modernised, and pit-head baths had done away with the tin baths once part of the equipment of a miner's home.

As an example of the handicap of traffic, once we were driving along a main road built up with houses, and passed a small lorry with a large pair of scales hanging down behind. The owner was a coal hawker selling coal by the hundredweight, once commonplace but now an anachronism. Because of the traffic we were unable to stop anywhere near to take a photograph. Prior to the First World War, coal cost 9d a hundredweight.

For one reason or another we often visited Hunslet, a suburb of Leeds, and formerly the site of potteries, of which the Leeds Pottery, now gone, had been the most famous. But here were the great engineering works, some of them, such as the Airedale Works, gone, but through a friend related to the owner we were shown round the Hunslet Engine Company's works by John Alcock, who as he told us had pioneered diesel engines, and had despatched locomotives all over the world. Speaking of Germany as a rival, he said 'we were the railway people for over 100 years'. Manual skills had changed to machine skills in his lifetime. Here too were T F and J H Braime whose giant works began with the invention of the oil can, which makes machines go all over the world; and Proctor Bros, wiremakers for the textile industry, who also marketed the Little Nipper Mouse trap stocked by every ironmonger's shop in England. Here also we found a sadler's shop and, although his wife thought that we were wasting his time, Tom Sinclair brimmed over with recollections of when 'Hunslet was Hunslet'. 'They were all poor people living in poor conditions but they were happy. Old Hunslet had a spirit like in the war.' His descriptions of food (oven-bottom cakes), taws (marbles), running with an iron hoop all over Leeds, and the comic bands playing mouth organs and penny whistles, were superb.

As if to overcome the environment, hobbies, clubs and games flourished. Music, of course, from brass bands to choral societies was and still is dominant above all. People loved 'a good sing', and concerts in chapels were full to capacity. Chrysanthemum shows were social events. Manufacturers had orchid houses and conservatories for exotic plants, and miners had greenhouses. Marie's family had a friend, a coal merchant, with whom they went botanising, and who sowed wild flower seeds on railway embankments. Pigeons and canaries drew others. We had a photograph sent of a kitchen interior of the early 1900s taken by a miner, whose son wrote a description of the complicated processes then required. Games such as knur and spell and arrow-throwing were played out of doors, and at night people sat on their doorsteps chatting with neighbours. Life was not all work.

At the end of our first year in December 1973, we sent a synopsis of the book and photographs to Dents, to the new head of editorial, Malcolm Gerratt, who we had already met and who we came to know well. The contract was signed for 'Life and Tradition in Industrial West Yorkshire' in March 1974. Again we were told that production costs for a heavily illustrated book had risen prodigiously, and an advance of £500 was offered, with lower royalties. In September we were disappointed when the number of photographs was reduced to some 150, of which, as it eventually turned out, 101 were old and forty-six taken by Marie. In addition there were to be only a few drawings, chiefly because the material did not lend itself. Also, because sizes of paper were being rationalised, the book was to be slightly smaller than the other two.

In 1974 there was still another year's work ahead. We visited a rhubarb farm in February, when the sticks were being gathered by candle-light in the dark, low sheds, and in March found one of the old potteries, once numerous in West Yorkshire, making use of the available clay and coal. Plant pots now formed the main trade, whereas once little models of cradles, chests of drawers, rocking chairs, plus puzzle jugs were produced — a form of folk art. It was in May that we attended the North of England Tulip Society Show at Wakefield, and admired the old English tulips resembling those seen in Dutch flower paintings. We also penetrated into the Holme Valley to find much of interest, and one of the last finds in late October was to seek out organ builders who allowed us to photograph the skilled men making and tuning the pipes.

Staying in the Colne Valley in August, we found the Saddleworth district an exhilarating drive over the hills, passing relics of the early textile trade. Near Delph we were shown beautiful printed shawls made in the early years of the last century in little mills by the Buckley family, and exported to Lisbon for the Spanish market. They illustrated the range of goods made in the past and also in the present in the mills. At Delph, too, we sought out the quarry where bakestones were dug and fired, for the home-baking of oatcake, carried round for sale in sacks, and tracked down two photographs of the bakestone makers dating from about 1910. Elsewhere we learnt more of the commercial baking of oatcake, once with as many as forty bakers in Bradford. The last at Haworth finished in 1975, and the equipment is preserved at Keighley Museum.

Our contract specified delivery of the manuscript by 1st November 1975. An extra task had been the transcriptions of the tapes, a tedious business undertaken by Joan. Pressed for time, we had refused a few speaking engagements, except for a luncheon organised by the Skipton branch of the Association of Yorkshire Bookmen, and in November 1974 we were asked by Kirklees Council to a literary dinner at Huddersfield, to celebrate the eightieth birthday of Phyllis Bentley. We managed to keep to our date. In September 1976 we spoke at a conference of Folk Life Studies at York on 'Hearth, Cooking and Peat'.

The book was published in November 1976 at £7.50, another increase. Reviews were extensive and favourable. In *The Times Educational Supplement* it was described as 'a marvellous book'. Many commented on the readability, and good production. Some reviewers were hooked on pre-conceived ideas rather than commenting on what we had garnered. Another said that the book was all the more interesting for not being 'a tedious idolising of the working class and denigration of the bosses'. One reviewer in the *Geographical Magazine* mistook its purpose and was out to pick holes.

We signed books and spoke at three literary luncheons and a dinner. One on 17th November 1976 was a *Yorkshire Post* event at the Majestic at Harrogate at which one of our fellow speakers was Frankie Howerd who told a blue joke, and arranged a flashlight to shine on his face. Two others, in December of the same year, were organised by *Yorkshire Ridings* magazine at Leeds and at Kershaw House, Calderdale. As we have said, we never professed to be good off-the-cuff speakers, but we passed muster. Through these particular events we came to know Dents' publicity lady, Liz Newlands, who later stayed with us to visit Haworth Parsonage. Later, in May 1977 we were invited to speak at a literary luncheon for the Spen Valley Festival of Creativity at Cleckheaton, organised by a friend, Chris Sumner. The main speaker was Dr Schumacher of 'Small is Beautiful' fame, and we were asked in order to promote our book *Life and Tradition in West Yorkshire.*

Within a few years of finishing this book, the textile industry of West Yorkshire collapsed. Takeovers abounded, mills closed down and chimneys were felled. The state of the pound and interest rates compounded to decimate exports, and as mills closed their machinery was sold cheaply to what in fact were rivals in the far East. Imports from these countries with cheap labour captured the market. Capital was required for new machinery, and for new fibres. In time two great mills, Salts at Saltaire and Dean Clough Mills at Halifax, fell empty and were bought by entrepreneurs and divided into individual units, workshops, retail outlets, restaurants, art galleries etc. At Manningham Mills, Listers were taken over by enterprising men with vision, and operate now with other mills elsewhere, but only in one part of the huge mill. Other firms, on the whole those making high-class goods, survived. In November 1976, Guy Crowther wrote in a letter: 'You have saved in words and pictures the story of a way of life which soon would have gone into oblivion'.

A DECADE OF ACHIEVEMENT

When in 1972 we had a respite before starting on West Yorkshire, we found that any available space — a two-storeyed small barn and two rooms in a house we owned at the time — were packed with the bygones collected for *Life and Tradition in the Yorkshire Dales*. Something had to be done about them. They had been carefully preserved, cleaned and treated for rust and woodworm, and a detailed stockbook had been kept, mostly compiled by Joan, giving the date acquired and the provenance of all the items. So that year we came to the decision to offer the whole collection to the then North Riding County Council for a public museum, believing that private ones, such as one at Leyburn that had been dispersed in 1941, had no guarantee of continuity.

Looking back now and seeing a well-established museum in the goods warehouse of the old station at Hawes, it is hard to think of all the trials and tribulations that brought this about. In the first place there was no curator to contact, only the Libraries, Archives and Museums committee of the county council, and it was Miss D M Hudson, the head librarian, who organised the visit of a group of county councillors to view the 382 items, some in groups. Word came through that they accepted the gift, but that there were no suitable premises available.

In 1974 the whole collection was moved from our buildings to those of the old offices of the Aysgarth District Council, then defunct, at Hawes, and for this Miss Hudson sent up a fleet of library vans, a memorable day. Meanwhile the curator of the Yorkshire Museum at York, T M Clegg, was appointed curator of the embryo museum at Hawes. Lack of premises and of funds intervened, and almost wrecked the project. However, in 1977, the Yorkshire Dales National Park, who had bought the station at Hawes, offered the goods warehouse, and money, then very tight, supplemented by grant aid, was found. Several county councillors, notably Colonel R J L Jackson, the then chairman, had felt that the county had an obligation to honour the scheme. W T C Walker, the county architect, and Roger Simpson, designer, were brought in, and we supplied information for wall boards and negatives for photographs.

When Michael Clegg and three technicians from York arrived to set up the museum in March 1979, we were allowed to help with labels and advice. Throughout Michael's stint as curator, we enjoyed a particularly harmonious relationship with both him and his assistant Peter Hall. We also came to know his wife, Pat Clegg, curator of the Harrogate Museums. A grand opening, attended by many dignitaries and donors, took place on 30th March 1979. It was an exhilarating time.[1]

Improvements were made when funds were available — for instance a new heating system was installed — and we gathered up further gifts which were offered to a

[1] For further information see *Origins of the Upper Dales Folk Museum* available at the musuem.

Michael Clegg and technicians setting up the museum in March 1979.

The opening of the Upper Dales Folk Museum, as it was then called, in March 1979. From left to right: W E Lockwood, Marie Joan and Colonel F J L Jackson.

new museum. Valuable mining tools, lead troughs and other treasures were donated and came from the Bolton Castle Museum, which was disbanded at this time, and in 1980 large cases arrived in which to display the knitting sheaths, gloves, wool combs and so on of the hand-knitting industry, now an important feature. Very many people gave help freely. For instance Jim Alderson of Stone House, Keld, offered to cut and dry peats for us to complete the display of a peat barrow, peat coup and peat spades. We were appalled when he said that the peats must be cut and dried out of sight of the lonely road at the head of Swaledale, as people passing in cars might steal them. J E Utley from Calderdale brought over a sackful of wooden soles, an iron ring and a diagram of a wooden horse for making clog soles.

In August 1982, at a public meeting, the Friends of the Upper Dales Folk Museum was started by Michael Clegg. Soon after that he retired to take up work as a television presenter. A genial man, with a sharp wit which amused us, he was admirably cut out for such a position. Appointed chairman and vice-chairman of the Friends, we took on fresh work arranging lectures, outings, fund-raising events and conducting parties round the museum. All were enjoyable.

One evening was devoted to dialect, when true dialect speakers the Rev James Alderson, Albert Alderson, from Stone House, and David Hall, born in Wensleydale, recited dialect poems. In July 1983 a garden party held at our cottage, for which

The Friends of the Upper Dales Folk Museum visiting Jervaulx Abbey.

The garden party at Coleshouse in 1983, for the Friends.

we had willing co-operation, raised £500 for funds. In April 1985 members of the British Agricultural History Society arrived, and we renewed our acquaintance with a distinguished scholar in the field of agriculture, Dr Joan Thirsk, and met Dr M I Ryder, author of *Sheep and Man*, with whom we discussed transhumance. The group was brought by our friend and neighbour, Christine Hallas, who had achieved a doctorate from the Open University, and who was on the committee of the society. Eventually new curators came and went, and the title was altered to the Dales Countryside Museum.

In 1984 the Friends raised £3,000 in aid of a link building between the goods warehouse and the main platform buildings, which would substantially increase space for displays. However, the National Park stepped in — the actual premises were of course their property — and claimed the link building as an information centre and shop. We were disappointed, and considered, as others people did, that we had raised money under false pretences. By now hardly a week passed without our having to attend to museum business. It was not our main interest, and we were getting older. At the annual general meeting in August 1988, we tendered our resignations, were made joint founder presidents, and each given bouquets of flowers. Others then assumed the responsibility of helping to carry through the ambitious plans in the pipeline.

One day in 1972 a small delegation from our own village came to see us. For two previous years an Askrigg Festival had been inaugurated by the vicar, the Rev Malcolm Stonestreet, and a small committee with Michael Weatherald as chairman ran it. This year the event was to last from 25th to 29th May, and although musical programmes

An outing of the Friends of the Museum to Burtersett Quarries, led by David Hall.

had been arranged, plans for an exhibition had fallen through. The delegation had come to enquire whether we could suggest anyone to fill the gap. They did not ask us to provide the exhibition. However, seeing our way to mounting one, we proposed a show of our work, with photographs, pictures, drawings and a display of bygones then in store. They agreed to this wholeheartedly.

The main room of our village hall is large and well-lit, and a number of screens were available. Including work by Ella Pontefract and Marie, we had between us written fourteen books, and planned to hang the illustrations in sections round the titles. A retired master from Yorebridge Grammar School, a keen amateur photographer, Alan Meadows, not only helped with the hanging, but enlarged and mounted many of Marie's best photographs. Hanging pictures is very tiring, and we remember us all getting exhausted. An additional display of local documents was loaned from the County Record Office, and the music in church, especially a concert rendering of *The Marriage of Figaro*, was first-rate. It was a successful co-operative village event, and we are reminded of it by a visitor's book with names and photographs which was given to us at the end. On the initiative of Mr Oliver, the whole exhibition went on to the premises of the *Yorkshire Post* in Leeds. We went there taking our friend Frank Shields, plumber and tinsmith, who figured in the photographs. In a writer's life the publication of each book marks a milestone on the way, and an exhibition of one's work is both a landmark and a kind of summing up.

1977 was Jubilee Year, and events at Askrigg outshone those of larger places. A pageant of village history, inspired by that performed in 1944, featured every main

An exhibition of our work at the 1972 Askrigg Festival in the village hall.

phase from Early Britons to the Coming of the Railway, and was relished by all. In addition a record book of photographs and a little information about every household in the village and the surrounding hamlets was compiled by a small committee. Partly the project aimed to obtain an idea of where everyone had come from, if they were not born in the village. A large half-leather-bound volume, similar to that for the WI scrapbook of 1965, made an album. In 1990 a group embarked on a similar venture with photographs and captions. The scrapbook and the two record books, much prized and kept in the village, reveal the composition of the inhabitants of Askrigg undertaken in an era of great change. In time they will be regarded as valuable historical documents.

Meanwhile, as a result of the publication of many books and articles, letters from many people poured in. We have filed most of them. Some were from admirers, some from students seeking help, some from individuals compiling family trees, and some offering information. Looking through one file we found the following written by Clarice Bray, neé Rule, from Camborne, Cornwall:

> I am the daughter of one of the Cornish lead-miners, but although Cornish, very much Yorkshire. Dad came home from gold-mining in Brazil to find a slump work-wise in Cornwall, [whence he took us] to live at West Gate, Weardale [where] he worked at Heights Quarry, taking food for the week in a bolster cover, and returning for a weekend stay ... When we went to live in Swaledale I was seven years old. The prospecting for lead was on a small scale, and working in really shocking conditions for about £4 a week. I well remember the night a man was killed in Old Gang, Yorkie Sunter of High Whitaside, who used to

A guided tour of Askrigg for the Friends of the Museum, given by Marie in 1993.

> take the trucks in the mine workings pulled by a pony, and the pony bolted trapping him ...
>
> We all attended the Congregational Chapel at Low Row. My father was in the choir singing in a tenor voice. What a great life we had with the Sunday School trip to Redcar and choir outing to Blackpool. There was Milk and Spice cake day, a sports day at Rowleth Bottom, rounded off in September with Reeth Show.

In April 1976 we had lunch in London with the new head of editorial at Dents, Malcolm Gerratt, who, knowing that we had a large collection of old photographs of Yorkshire, was considering the idea of a book of them. However, a director of the firm discovered a collection covering all England, and we were dropped for the time being. Eventually Dents no longer wished to reprint *Yorkshire Cottage* (published in 1942) and *Life and Tradition in the Yorkshire Dales.* They suggested a publisher for the latter in the Midlands with whom they had links, but it so happened that David Joy, then in charge of the publication of books at the *Dalesman,* called as he did from time to time, and, discussing the matter with him, we decided that we had better stick to a publisher we knew and one near at hand, so we chose the *Dalesman.* When this firm reprinted *Yorkshire Cottage* in 1984, we were disappointed with the cheap reproduction of a book long cherished by many people. On the other hand their paperback edition of *Life and Tradition* was well printed. We have always appreciated good production, for which Dents were noted.

We had already started on a new book, because when in London in 1977 we had worked at the Guildhall on documents relating to Crown property in Wensleydale in the seventeenth century, and we had begun reading the early newspaper, the *Wensleydale Advertiser*, printed at Hawes, a daunting task. Our new idea, eventually to be called *A Dales Heritage*, drew on the mass of material accumulated over forty years of work in the Dales. Some of the manuscripts in our archives had been given to us, some had been bought at sales, and some had been lent and notes taken from them. A large proportion related to Swaledale and to lead-mining. For instance, there was a letter-book compiled by Matthew Wadeson, lead agent, of Stockton-on-Tees, which took about three months to decipher and make sense of, and involved a visit to Stockton, an unusual and interesting town with quays alongside the river, where pigs of lead from Old Gang mines used to be stored.

One delightful study was based on the pocket diaries kept from 1898 to 1955 by a gamekeeper and friend of long standing, Harry Storey of Askrigg, lent by his daughter Peg Scarr. They touched on many aspects of Dales life and recorded a period of great change. Other friends, such as Calvert Chapman, the Askrigg blacksmith who had made the ironwork for our cottage, and his relations at Gunnerside, lent old ledgers, from which we gained a picture of the life of David Calvert (1819-1906), blacksmith of Gunnerside, who lived through the desperate times when the mines were closing.

Another chapter gave a profile of the Rev John Dupont, vicar of Aysgarth from 1733 to 1768. Through the Rev C White, a former vicar of the parish, we made contact with his descendants, Charles Dupont of Montreal and his daughter, Lady Cunyngham of Banbury, who spent the day with us to look at Temple Farm, formerly the home of John Dupont, between Aysgarth and West Witton. We also had lent to us the Garth Diaries by Frances Garth of Crackpot, for the study of which we had the advantage of knowing Frances, who died in 1970. She was one of the daughters of Francis Garth, yeoman farmer. Frances had spent some time at the Slade School in London, and we have photographs of her portraits of her sister Mary.

In the first section of the book we used all our accumulated knowledge to describe the Oxnop Valley, the hinterland of our cottage at Askrigg, and in the last, our favourite wild region of the Dales, from Keld to the Cumbrian border. The first kept us in touch with our friends, the Porters of Low Oxnop, and the last with our other friends, the Aldersons, formerly of Stone House, but now at Keld. We were introduced to the landlords of Stone House, from Slough, who we met and who lent us documents, thus providing rare new material. Half the photographs for the book were taken by Marie and the rest lent. One friend, Edmund Cooper, who we had known for many years, and who wrote *Muker: The Story of a Yorkshire Parish* and other valuable studies of Swaledale, lent us two or three photographs. He was a kind and generous man who, after a working life elsewhere, had returned to Swaledale, the home of his fore-elders.

In the midst of work on this book in July 1979, Joan fell seriously ill with an attack of shingles. At that time remedies were limited and it was a painful time. On 4th November of that year Marie wrote in her diary 'Five months since shingles started'.

Side effects meant a small operation to a misplaced nerve in the arm, and weekly physiotherapy in hospital during 1980. As a result more work, including the typing, fell on Marie and delayed completion.

Dents had felt that the book was too local for their list, and so on 16th November 1982 the *Dalesman* published it after the usual difficulty over the choice of title. Bill Mitchell (former editor of the magazine) had at last chosen it, we were told. The book was a success, for it was reprinted in 1984. A review in the *Yorkshire Post* by Gordon Forster of Leeds University did it justice, saying that the essays were 'case studies of the commonplace of a way of life now lost', and David Morgan Rees wrote a long and appreciative review in *Yorkshire Life*. It pleased us to be able to put on record so much new material about favourite places.

On 26th March 1985, David Joy called on us to discuss a kind of sequel to *A Dales Heritage*, which we had already embarked on. He suggested a similar format and length. Again we had unused material in our files from various sources. Of considerable value were transcripts from the Public Record Office, either gleaned from our own visits long ago or sent to us by our agent, Nellie McNeil O'Farrell. One lot referred to the loss of the deer in the Dales, and the other to the troubles associated with corn mills on the River Dee in Dentdale. Further sections focused on barns, mountain sheep, emigrants, and a collection of life stories.

We look back with pleasure on the fieldwork necessary for the study of barns and sheep undertaken in the summer of 1985. The great barn at Bolton Abbey, the largest in the Dales, points to monastic times, as do other great barns, some formerly at Kilnsey, a grange of Fountains Abbey. Cruck barns near Archway Farm, at Drebley in Wharfedale, and handsome early barns at Lawkland, one of which has since been pulled down, were highlights of our search. Barns, a threatened species because of new farming methods, decorate the landscape of the Dales, and, similarly constructed to houses, exhibit the skill and pride in work of the men who built them. Exploring for barns and deer took us to Appletreewick, where the Mason family, amongst other help, took us in a Land Rover over the moors to see Agill, a true longhouse on Barden Moor, at the top of the Valley of Desolation. William Mason produced a treasure, a small old photograph of this from a wallet in his pocket, and we had it copied. It was a memorable day of exploration.

For sheep we learnt of transhumance, the movement of sheep from winter to summer pasturage and vice versa, practiced in the Middle Ages, and described to us by George Siddall and Richard Fawcett, who from the head of Wensleydale had organised the movement of flocks of sheep to the Lake District for winter grazing. In Littondale we made new friends, the Cowans, who readily offered help, and renewed our acquaintance with the Ingleby family, who had left their home at Nether Hesleden, but who well remembered sending sheep from there to Nidderdale. It was the wedding of Christopher Ingleby of Halton Gill, nephew of Guy Ingleby of Nether Nesleden, which Ella Pontefract and Marie Hartley attended in the 1930s whilst working on the book on Wharfedale. As a result of these contacts, we borrowed for copying and reproduction a fine collection of sheep photographs. At that time we had by

Handing over the manuscript of Dales Memories *to David Joy, editor of the* Dalesman, *at Ribblehead in 1985.*

Joan, Bill Mitchell (former editor of the Dalesman*) and Marie near Hill Top Tarn, upper Swaledale.*

chance seen the photographic work of Mary Farnell of Clapham, who became a friend, and thenceforward took on the copying of old photographs and enlarging of our negatives.

The chapter on emigrants drew on many threads, foremost perhaps the Dalesmen who had gone to Winsconsin in the 1840s, but also another family, the Terrys, who left for Tasmania. One, Abigail Curkeet of Mount Horeb, Winsconsin, wrote to us to ask permission to quote from our book *Yorkshire Village* which she had found in the library at the University at Madison, and she eventually sent us the result of her researches into the Dinsdales and others who hailed from Askrigg in the form of a thick paperback called *The Circuit Rider*. It was a marvellous compilation, from which we quoted liberally. Another correspondent in Winsconsin, Jane Metcalfe Caygill, revealed by her very name her origins; for these are familiar Dales names. These contacts eventually brought friends from that state to Askrigg to be welcomed by many people who found themselves related, and who, including us, still keep up with each other.

As for the life stories, we had most of them in hand, and only required permission to publish them. But for one, John Swales (1874-1975), we sought out his daughter, Jane Calvert, in an isolated farm near Pateley Bridge. Mrs Calvert treasured several of our early books, some bygones such as her mother's knitting stick, and remembered the harshness of her father's early life. When *Dales Memories* was published and we took her a copy, she was very moved. Bitter struggles to find work or make a living are recorded for posterity in these stories.

By now, publishers favoured colour photographs for their book wrappers. Based on one of her own photographs, Marie, improving on it, painted an acrylic picture of sheep being driven up the road from Arncliffe in Littondale to Malhamdale, and this, approved for the wrapper, was bought by David Joy for himself. The book was published in September 1986 in paperback form, with an additional 500 hardback copies which had to be signed. The hardback at £10.95 was hardly expensive, yet it sold slowly. Again Gordon Forster wrote appreciatively in the *Yorkshire Post*. We were especially pleased with a letter from Lord James, former vice-chancellor of the University of York, who wrote: 'I know few writers who can make solid research and scholarship so immensely readable for the ordinary reader, and give him new eyes, eg to look at barns with fresh interest and understanding. I envy and congratulate you'.

At intervals over the years we have contributed articles to the *Dalesman*, usually at the request of the editor. Once we were walking to Hill Top Tarn at the head of Swaledale, prospecting for a Friends of the Museum outing, when a man appearing in the distance turned out to be Bill Mitchell, editor of the *Dalesman*. In 1988 he retired, and a television programme devoted to his twenty years in office marked the event. Our recollections recorded for this harked back to the start of the magazine in 1939 by Harry Scott. David Joy then took over as editor. The following year a buffet lunch at Clapham celebrated fifty years of publication of the magazine, attended by many contributors and fellow editors. It was an enjoyable occasion.

TWO ALBUMS

Opening the post starts our working day, as it must for other people, especially the self-employed. The news that letters bring may be many things. It may be innocuous, it may give information, it may bring bad tidings, it may affect the schedule of the day ahead, and it may on very rare occasions be startling. One such startling letter arrived in January 1986 from the vice-chancellor of the University of York, Berrick Saul, inviting us to accept the honorary degrees of Master of the University. The conferment itself took place on a fine summer's day in July. It was not too alarming, as we were allocated a ceremony before a large congregation of staff, guests and students, who themselves received their degrees. Dr W Shiels gave the address, emphasising our pioneer work on traditional life, and saying 'that their names, like those of Marks and Spencer, trip naturally from the tongue'. The Chancellor, Lord Swan, throughout a benign presence, conferred our degrees.

Still another startling letter came in March 1986, when Malcolm Gerratt wrote from Dents commissioning us to compile a book of old photographs of Yorkshire.

The degree ceremony at the University of York in 1986: Lord Swan in the centre and Dr W Shiels on the right.

It was a reversal of their decision of a year or two ago. The book was allotted a short text and 300 black-and-white photographs dating from 1900 to 1950, and it was planned to be published in 1987, the centenary year of the publishing house of Dent. From another department at Dents we were asked to have the copyright of each photograph cleared by a letter. This we could see was impossible for hundreds of photographs, and we refused to comply.

Although we were still involved with some work on *Dales Memories*, we readily agreed to this interesting commission. It has to be said that only our hard-won knowledge of Yorkshire and of likely people to contact, gained over many years, made such a book possible. Again we had to cover all Yorkshire, and again stayed away in various locations to visit libraries, museums, friends and relations. We divided the book into five sections, with an introduction to each set of photographs. Not only were these carefully chosen to represent all aspects of Yorkshire life, but we wanted the captions to be comprehensive.

Our own collection of photographs was inadequate, but we found fifty of Marie's taken with the old Rolleiflex (she had two) when writing *Yorkshire Tour* with Ella Pontefract in the late 1930s, and several more from family albums. One from the 1930s was of pea-picking by a gang of thirty or forty women in the Selby district, a job nowadays undertaken by machines. Another was of a Humber keel with its large sail reflected in the waters of the Ouse, a vessel now gone. From an album of the Ripley Pageant of 1930, Joan found one of her father and mother dressed in seventeenth century costume. Another from the archives depicted Harold and Artie Hodgson in their guise as chimney sweeps, although in summer they kept donkeys on the sands at Scarborough.

We remember with pleasure our visits to libraries and museums, where librarians and curators often put themselves out to help. One was Mrs Ann Heap of the local studies department of Leeds Central Library, who procured for us photographs of working class Leeds; Philip Brown of Beverley Library had postcards of what, to us, were unusual events in the East Riding; Philip van Riel sent us a photograph of girls making Pontefract cakes by hand. From Doncaster, Terry Manby took great trouble, and passed on our request to Cusworth Hall Museum, which sent us a photograph of a miner's family with a charming story attached for the caption. At the Harrogate Museum, Pat Clegg sent information about Spurn Point, for Michael Clegg was president of the Yorkshire Naturalists, who had bought the peninsular.

The largest number of photographs came from Raymond Hayes of Hutton-le-Hole, who we had met and made friends with in our work on *Life in the Moorlands of North-East Yorkshire*. In all we used twenty-four of his own and his father's photographs of York, Scarborough and the moorlands. A favourite from there was a picture of a waggonette drawn by two horses taking visitors for a drive along a moorland road near Hutton. John Edenbrow, the photographer, found us excellent Leeds scenes, and C H Wood of Bradford lent us some children's period pieces. Underground photographs of coal-mines proved difficult to obtain, although P T Heathfield, secretary of the National Union of Mineworkers, responded to our request and said that he knew our work. The best underground photograph came via the *Yorkshire Post*, of Dodsworth Miners Welfare Band playing at the pit bottom.

Then, we found that a few personal friends had large collections of old photographs. For instance Chris Sumner of Hightown, near Cleckheaton, then chairman of the Brontë Society, came up with several, one a chapel sewing party with the ladies sitting round a table, all wearing lace caps. Brian Arundel co-operated with school scenes from both Ackworth School and one at Batley. David and June Hall of Bainbridge helped with a rare photograph of visitors in Edwardian times at Gordale Scar, a picture of three little boys on a horse from Marsett near Semerwater, and a family group from Hooton Pagnell, South Yorkshire, with a good story attached. Quite by chance through a mutual friend we came to know Nan Alcock of Cawood, and learnt from her neighbours much about the traffic of barges on the River Ouse and the fishing of salmon in a river unfamiliar to us.

Another most fortunate find occurred when we visited our friends the Gatenbys near Rudston. Taking up our request for photographs with enthusiasm, Bill Gatenby contacted P E Atkinson, who discovered a set of Wold scenes owned by a Mrs Hague. As far as we remember, they had only recently been found and sent north from London. We used eight, and with others from the Wolds thus preserved a remarkable record of waggons and horses, ploughing and threshing days. Also, when we were writing *Life in the Moorlands* we had been recommended to visit a C R Dykes who lived at Brawby in the Vale of Pickering. He was a poorly man, who nevertheless was pleased to talk to us about his early life as a plough boy, and lent us to copy two photographs, one of himself at sixteen with his three horses, and another of a threshing set being drawn by a shaft horse and six pairs of horses at Wharram-le-Street on the Wolds.

These incomplete notes give some idea of the work involved in the book. All along, too, Mary Farnell, our photographer friend, had been kept busy copying old photographs, and had even found one or two suitable ones from the Clapham district. Copyright was cleared without undue trouble. Marie, who was too preoccupied to keep more than a sketchy diary, wrote: 'It was far harder work than one can imagine'. In fact we have more letters, notes, reviews and so on filed for this book than for many others.

Meanwhile, on 27th May 1988 bad tidings came through — Dents had succumbed to the takeover fever afflicting the publishing world, which was changing altogether from the one we had known. Started in 1888 by Joseph Mallaby Dent, the firm had become one of the renowned family houses of publishing, for as well as having an outstanding general list, it inaugurated the Everyman's Library in 1905. Alas in 1988, there was no direct descendant of the family to carry on. But Dents was to continue under the new owners, Weidenfeld and Nicolson, as a separate firm with its own books. Takeovers are disastrous for authors for several reasons, not least for personnel changes. We heard from Liz Newlands almost at once that she was leaving, and the publication of *Yorkshire Album* was delayed from spring to autumn.

Also, on 31st May 1988 paragraphs illustrated with Marie's work appeared in the 'People' column of the *Yorkshire Post*, quoting from Sotheby's catalogue that nearly

200 illustrations from our books were to be auctioned in June. Together with many others from Dent books, they had come from a general clearance unconnected with the current company. We telephoned Sothebys stating that these were not Dents to sell, and found that others were claiming the same. Eventually we were assured that everything would be withdrawn, and returned to us, as they were in due course. But it was an anxious time.

According to our contract, the text and photographs of *Yorkshire Album* were due at Dents on 1st April 1988, and when the time came they were regarded as so precious that we met Malcolm Gerratt and his assistant, Anna Wyn, at the Royal Station Hotel at York, and handed over the parcel. After lunch there, we should have enjoyed an afternoon with them in York, but the heavens opened, and in deluges of rain we left for home.

Later that month we were invited to lunch at the Wensleydale Ladies Luncheon Club, when Robert Rutt, Bishop of Leicester, was speaking on 'Knitting'. He had recently published *A History of Hand-Knitting*, a worldwide knowledgeable survey, beginning with a chapter 'Before 1500' and ending at the present day. We took a pair of mittens knitted by a famous Dent knitter, Mary Allen, to show him and enjoyed the talk immensely. In his introduction to his book, referring to *The Old Hand-Knitters of the Dales*, he paid us the best compliment we have ever had, by writing, 'They have written only one book on knitting, but its influence has been great and good'.

Yorkshire Album, subtitled 'Photographs of Everyday Life', was published at £14.95 on 18th August 1988. Malcolm Gerratt sent us 'the finished book' hoping that we should like it. The photographs were well arranged and well reproduced, which was all-important. On the whole, reviews were good if not widespread — *The Sunday Times* printed the chimney sweep photograph with a caption, and the *Yorkshire Evening Press* a long notice by our friend of long standing, Ron Willis. The book appeared twice as a bestseller, once at the top in the *Yorkshire Post*. In the *Darlington and Stockton Times*, our local paper, we took exception to a scrappy review and the words 'trawled through' to describe our extensive search.

What we did enjoy were radio interviews and signing sessions accompanied by lavish displays at bookshops. At York, Dents' new publicity lady came from London to look after us at Claude Gill's new bookshop, and at Leeds, Austicks put on a prominent display, as did Andrew Sharpe at the Grove Bookshop at Ilkley. In September, when we were staying for a holiday at the Expanse Hotel at Bridlington, we signed books at Fawcetts bookshop at Driffield for Christine Clubley, who had taken us up, and there met many friends from the Wolds. Dr Ian and Mrs Stead from the British Museum, then excavating prehistoric burials at Garton-on-the-Wolds, bought two books, and one day we saw their new find, a chariot burial. Later a paperback edition of *Yorkshire Album* was published, and eventually two or three hundred copies of this were remaindered, something that would not have happened in former days.

In the autumn of 1988 two pleasant happenings occurred. At a ceremony at the Folk Museum, the Yorkshire Dales Society made us their first honorary life members. The society guards the interests and the landscape of the Dales, and prints a

Signing copies of Yorkshire Album *at Austicks bookshop, the Headrow, Leeds, in 1988.*

quarterly review giving a programme of events and up-to-date information. The second was a comprehensive profile of us written by David Morgan Rees for the *Countryman*. We remember, too, a little later, an invitation to attend a buffet lunch to celebrate the twenty-first anniversary of the formation of the Skipton Bookmen, attended by Bill Mitchell and David Joy of the *Dalesman*, where we remembered speaking to them many years ago.

There was an obvious sequel to *Yorkshire Album* — a similar book on the Dales. We put the idea to Dents in March 1989. They took it up with enthusiasm and proposed a book of 15,000 words, 200 black-and-white and about twenty-five colour photographs, to be completed by 31st December 1989. We began work at once as before sorting out suitable photographs, and chose 126 of Marie's and some from our archives, which made a good start. Again we planned a framework of seven sections, and, as we say in the preface, one or two photographs had to represent the subject, for instance castles, seventeenth-century houses and family groups.

1989 was a fine, hot summer, and day by day we set out to visit all the Dales. On the whole, friends rather than libraries and museums came up with what we wanted. New friends in Malhamdale were Frank and Florence Carr, who, like the Masons at Appletreewick, took us on a tour in their Land Rover to look at dewponds, old houses at Bordley, and to their neighbours at Park House. Frank has died since then, but we

Some of the many friends we have made over the years, and who have helped us in our work: (top left) George and Mary Ellison of Greenwell, Dent; (top right) William and Mary Mason of Appletreewick, Wharfedale; (below) Florence and Frank Carr, with Joan on Malham Moor.

still keep in touch. In Dentdale we found treasure trove in a box of glass plates shown to us by our friends who we have already mentioned, George and Mary Ellison of Greenwell. We used seventeen of these. They were so precious that we took them straight to Clapham for copying and returned them ourselves. By chance, one day when we were at Greenwell the mobile library van arrived, and we took the opportunity of taking a photograph of that modern amenity. Similarly by chance we were passing Barden Tower as a refuse collecting van was emerging, and took a photograph, wondering what Lady Anne Clifford would have thought of it.

Miss N Cutcliffe Hyne of Kettlewell and Fred Willis of Aysgarth produced family photographs with good details for captions. Donald Wood of Bolton Abbey remembered the waggonettes that plied there, and John Blythe of Hawes, then an old man, enjoyed sharing his scrapbooks with us. At Richmond, Chris Alderson and his daughter, Eleanor, formerly of Black Howe, Keld, and once one of the Swaledale singers, lent us further photographs. At Middlesmoor in Nidderdale we were warmly welcomed, and sent on to Mr and Mrs J Haines at Bouthwaite. Although they were proposing to publish a book themselves on the building of the Scar House Reservoir, they lent us two photographs, and in return we advised them as best we could on compilation and publishing. A year or two later they turned up at our cottage at Askrigg with a splendid booklet on this engineering feat. It is impossible to do full justice to the collaboration which we received. Again Mary Farnell was kept busy copying old photographs.

We often discussed this book with David and June Hall, who were always ready to help, as we were with them. David suffered from ill-health, but nonetheless wrote a book on the Burtersett quarries, a history of the village of Bellerby, where they had lived, the story of a Quaker, Richard Robinson of Countersett, near Semerwater, and conducted classes on local history. We helped particularly with the Bellerby book, and attended a party to launch it. Alas David died aged fifty, in January 1991, a serious loss to local history.

But all was not well. We finished the book on 15th December 1989, and expected that, as with *Yorkshire Album*, we should meet up with Malcolm Gerratt at York to deliver the package, but time drifted on, and on 31st January 1990 we posted both text and photographs. Then, telephone calls broke the news that, due to the recession, reluctantly the colour photographs had to go, to be replaced with black-and-white. As we had taken trouble to muster unusual and attractive colour prints, this was to say the least disappointing. A further blow came in January 1991, when Malcolm wrote to say he was leaving Dents, being 'the only surviving member from the old team'. Authors were not the only ones to suffer from takeovers. Friendly and helpful new people filled the gaps in editorial, production and sales departments.

A Dales Album, subtitled 'A Pictorial History of the Yorkshire Dales', came out on 11th April 1991. It was again well reviewed. The *Northern Echo* included it in their bestseller list, and the *Yorkshire Post* review ended with 'Highly nostalgic, highly recommended'. It got off to a good start, but faded away. Poor marketing followed on from all the changes, troubles and delays, and for the salesmen involved the Dales were outside their beat. In 1994 copies were remaindered, for us an unwelcome experience, and a sad fate for a handsome, valuable book. A year or two earlier the whole group of Weidenfeld and Dent were taken over by the Orion Publishing Company, and by 1995 all the rights to publish our books had reverted to us. Sixty-one years of amicable, considerate and mutually enjoyable association ceased.

A SUMMING UP

In 1987 it was to be expected that many of our books would be out of print. The first dated back to the 1930s, and Dents had gradually shed them and others off, and had formally returned the rights to publication to us. The Dalesman Publishing Company had still kept *The Old Hand-Knitters* in print since 1951, and in 1961, as we have said, they were pleased to take on *Life and Tradition in the Yorkshire Dales*, issuing it as an attractive paperback. Reprinted in 1985 and 1989, this did well for them. Similarly, they produced *Yorkshire Cottage* in paperback in 1984. They also wished to consider a reprint of *Life in the Moorlands of North-East Yorkshire,* but time dragged on, and they dropped the idea.

In the normal course of events, one would think that this would be the end. But on 1st December 1987, we received a letter from Michael Wayte, a member of staff of a printing and small publishing firm recently formed in 1981 and based at Otley. Mr Wayte had been talking to a friend of ours at an antiquarian bookshop in Skipton, and had heard that we liked Smith Settle's good production. He was exploring the possibility of publishing some of our books, and soon proposed by letter paperback

Marie at work on a wood engraving.

Brian Settle and Ken Smith, partners in Smith Settle, printers and publishers.

editions of *Swaledale, Wensleydale* and *Wharfedale*, written by Ella Pontefract and Marie in the 1930s. We signed a contract for the three books in 1988. As typographic copyright had lapsed, they could be printed from the original pages. We supplied colour transparencies for the covers. The photographs in the old editions were omitted, and the wood engravings as sole illustrations came into their own. Mr Wayte sent us advance copies, saying how he had enjoyed handling them. He left the firm in February 1989. Some of the wood engravings were printed a little dark, a fault remedied in later editions. But the books were attractive and sold well.

To have a publisher within fifty miles or so allowed for easy communication, and at intervals Ken Smith, one of the partners of Smith Settle, came to see us. Starting a new publishing firm, he welcomed our names as established authors on his list and we benefitted accordingly. In March 1988 he had seen the wood engravings in the early Dales books, and, as he said himself, he was captivated by them.

A new project developed. On 5th May 1988 he brought Simon Lawrence with him to Askrigg. Simon was the owner of a private press, the Fleece Press, then based at Wakefield, and a member of a family who had supplied Marie with wood blocks and engraving tools in the 1930s. It was proposed that 250 copies of books of wood engravings be printed in three styles — one quarter-bound in cloth to be sold at £40, and a second quarter-bound in goatskin at £60, and the third fully-bound and with an additional set of engravings for £140. Simon was to print them by hand on an Albion Press from the original blocks which, kept in an outhouse, were in perfect condition, and Smith Settle was to do the binding.

Marie found a sheet of repeat prints of a small wood engraving for some of the covers. It took Simon three months to print, using dampened Velin Arches paper. The results were perfectly printed and handsomely bound books. To Marie they seemed the culmination of her work as an artist, and she does not forget Ken Smith's part in this. The special edition sold at once, and the rest quickly, some being bought to keep for their increase in value.

We were still engaged on *A Dales Album*, but on 10th November 1989 we found time to attend a reception at Austick's bookshop in Harrogate to launch the wood engraving books. We knew the Austick brothers, especially David, quite well, and they had always backed our work. Notabilities, relations and friends arrived, and we enjoyed the occasion. An appreciative account of it appeared in the 'People' column of the *Yorkshire Post* by Felicity McCormick. It was Felicity who had reported the advertised sale of our illustrations in Sotheby's catalogue, which earned our gratitude.

Meanwhile, Smith Settle took on reprints of *Yorkshire Village* in 1989, and *The Yorkshire Dales* in 1991, both attractively produced for £7.50 and £6.50 respectively. They also began exploring the possibility of reprinting *Life and Tradition in West Yorkshire* and *Life in the Moorlands of North-East Yorkshire*, both of which duly appeared in hardback and paperback form. Inevitably for all this, a thick file of letters built up, many from Mark Whitley, Ken's right-hand man. By 14th October 1991 they had sold out the first printing of *Yorkshire Village*, and Ken wrote: 'My faith in your work has been justified'.

But this was not all. In a letter dated 21st December 1989, Ken Smith had outlined the above, and in addition a new book, then to be called 'Yorkshire Sketchbook', to show Marie's artwork, and also another book of wood engravings, on the same lines as the first. Simon Lawrence, then fully committed, was booked for 1991.

The title 'Yorkshire Sketchbook' was later changed to *Forms and Colours*, and it included forty-six reproductions of Marie's oil paintings and watercolours, beginning with one painted in the late 1920s and finishing with one in 1988, plus a black-and-white section of wood engravings, pencil and pen-and-ink sketches. Some of the pencil drawings came from those made for the book *Yorkshire Tour*, written with Ella Pontefract in 1939. Little has been said in this book of the paintings, which were usually commissioned (or they would never have been done), and undertaken in between the books. 1977 seems to have been a productive year.

Transparencies of the paintings were required for production, and Ken sent up a photographer, Richard Littlewood, who came for the day early in July, bringing special equipment. He took photographs of each painting, brought together by us from local people in the morning and returned at night. It was a very exhausting day. For others not near at hand, several owners co-operated by sending transparencies of their pictures, and also Richard visited two or three homes round Leeds and Harrogate to photograph paintings. For the drawings Marie had partly to dismember her sketch books, which have never quite recovered. The book was published in October 1992, beautifully produced, except that some of the reproductions of the paintings were a little too pale.

For the second wood engraving book, there were still about the same number as

Anne and Fred Burkhardt with Jane, Fred's daughter, on the right, and a friend on the left, on holiday with us in Borrowdale.

before of chapter headings and tailpieces, but no large ones for the beginnings of each of three sections. By working on two old blocks of Oxnop and cotton grass, partially complete, Marie provided two, and for the third, the Wharfedale section, she found a wood block of the right size and a drawing of Bolton Abbey, and achieved an engraving in keeping with the rest. Eyesight, as one might suppose, did not fail her, but she feared over-working it. Review copies of all these books, both new and old, were despatched by Smith Settle and new reviews appeared, some long. A good one was written by Harry Mead in the *Northern Echo* on the three Dales books.

In the spring of 1991 we fell seriously ill with an attack of flu. Joan had to be rushed off to a nursing home where she suffered a slight stroke, and we both convalesced for a fortnight in a home in Harrogate. At this time we considered moving to Harrogate to be near our relations, and Coleshouse was put up for sale. However, we began to recover and to repent our decision, and the cottage was withdrawn. One relief was that we avoided the daunting task of moving all the accumulation of books, papers, documents, sketch books, artist's materials and so on, in addition to the normal goods of a household.

Because of illness, holidays were curtailed. Northumberland had been a favourite for some years, but now even Bridlington was too far away, and we spent breaks in the Lake District, one shared with the Burkhardts. Friends diminished, as they do as

Marie and Joan undertaking fieldwork at West Bolton Farm, Wensleydale, in 1992. The field behind them is Bakestone Bower.

one grows older. Many remembered local ones had died many years ago — friends who lived in a past age, who took to us and of whom we were fond. But others remained, and new ones were appreciated — the Gardners who, when Billy retired, came to live at Stone House near Sedbusk. The sister of his wife, Dorothy, had been Marie's best schoolfriend. Each Christmas we spent the day with them, until Billy's death in 1982, as we do now with Elvin and Elizabeth Berry, who retired to Reeth in 1986. Elizabeth had been the head of the West Yorkshire Archives Service, so that we had much in common.

A large part of 1992 was spent collecting together the artwork for *Forms and Colours*. But that year our friend, Ann Holubecki, daughter of Margaret Hopper already mentioned, showed us a farm account book kept in the last century by Henry King of West Bolton, a farm between Redmire and Carperby on the Bolton estate, and his son, William, who rented two farms in the Sleddale valley above Hawes. We saw its potential, and asked permission from the owner, Ann's brother-in-law, to study it with a view to writing a monograph. It turned out to be a protracted but enjoyable and fascinating piece of work.

We were supported by the farmer at West Bolton, John Amsden, Ann and Margaret Ritchie, a member of the King family, and especially by Michael Ashcroft, archivist at the County Record Office at Northallerton. Much could be read into the disjointed accounts of West Bolton — that corn was grown there in sufficient quantities to warrant the installation of a barn thresher worked by a water wheel fed by a dam. We had been alerted to this by our friend Fletcher Percival of Carperby, a farmer inter-

An exhibition entitled 'Forms and Colours with Documents', to which we contributed paintings and wood engravings, at the North Yorkshire County Record Office, Northallerton, in 1992.

ested in local history, and we were shown the dam by John Amsden on a tour of the farm. At the Record Office we learnt that the farmstead with others was built during a wave of improvement on the Bolton estate that altered the landscape of that part of Wensleydale. West Bolton and its neighbour, Castle Bank, are situated on the finest medieval landscape in the Yorkshire Dales, terraced extensively with the lynchets of the open field system. The essay, with illustrations, was published by the Record Office in one of their *Bulletins*.

For some time we had been considering what to do with the notes for all our books and the letters connected with them, kept in two four-drawer files, and our photographs taken and collected over many years. We discussed the matter with Elizabeth Berry, who suggested depositing them at Claremont, the rooms of the Yorkshire Archaeological Society, adding that it was a kind of tradition for members with valuable archives to do so. We hesitated for a long time, then wrote off to the secretary of the society. Late in 1992 the archivist, Sylvia Thomas, came to see what we had, and pronounced our filing system as 'exemplary'; also Mr J Telford, who was in charge of the photographic records at Claremont, came with his wife. So it was agreed that after our deaths, the files and photographs should all go to Leeds.

The 1990s were surprisingly punctuated with exhibitions. The first in 1991 was at Askrigg, where Marie was invited to exhibit paintings and wood engravings at the annual exhibition held in August of a group of artists living in and around the village. Marie for once enjoyed being part of a group. The second took place at the County

At the 1993 retrospective exhibition of our work entitled 'Reflections – Yorkshire as seen by Marie Hartley and Joan Ingilby'. From left to right: Mary Farnell, Joan, Elizabeth Berry and Marie, with Alan King behind.

Record Office in November 1992, entitled 'Forms and Colours with Documents'. The office has wall cases, ideal for displaying documents, and a very large foyer, and we lent paintings and wood engravings to illustrate the documents displayed. One was the original contract of 1378 for the building of Bolton Castle by John Lewyn for Sir Richard Scrope. It was an unusual and attractive display.

The third exhibition, 'Relief Prints by Yorkshire Artists', was held in June at Ingleborough Community Centre. Wood engravings and linocuts in variety were arranged under each artist's name round the walls of the exhibition hall. Marie's prints, surely brought into prominence by Smith Settle's publications, sold well. Then in 1993 the warden, Alan King, and Mary Farnell, a member of the committee, arranged and hung a retrospective exhibition of our work called 'Reflections — Yorkshire as seen by Marie Hartley and Joan Ingilby'. It was on similar lines to the exhibition at Askrigg in 1972, except that after over twenty years we had written and illustrated more books, so that there was more work to display. A painting of Marie's in colour, printed free by Smith Settle, made a poster worth keeping. The show was opened by Elizabeth Berry with a well-informed speech. Only some twenty miles from home, we and friends could easily go over to see and enjoy it. Two visitors were nephews of

Joan and Marie at the exhibition at the University Gallery, Leeds.

Ella Pontefract, one from Folkestone staying with his brother in Harrogate, and another was Dr Hilary Diaper, keeper of the University Gallery at Leeds, with whom we discussed the possibility of the whole show going on to Leeds.

Eventually a date was fixed for an exhibition at Leeds in 1994, and Hilary came to Askrigg in the autumn to choose the artwork. A fully bound catalogue with the title *A Favoured Land - Yorkshire in Text and Image* was printed by Smith Settle. It gave brief biographies and essays on our work by Gordon Forster, Dr Joan Thirsk and Hilary herself, as well as illustrated summaries of our books. The gallery does not have a formal opening, but on the first day a large company assembled, including the vice-chancellor, Dr Thirsk, Professor Beresford, Ken Smith, the new editor of the *Dalesman* Terry Fletcher, Ella Pontefract's nephews and many others.The show attracted praise for its contents and arrangement, and at the sales counter, usual there, many wood engravings were sold. It certainly was the climax of our four years of exhibitions.

Later on in 1994 there came through the post one of those startling pieces of news, rarely experienced. This time it was the proposed presentation to us of the Silver Medal of the Yorkshire Archaelogical Society, awarded for 'Outstanding contributions to the study of Yorkshire's past'. Only four had previously been given. The ceremony took place on 1st December 1993, at the society's rooms in Leeds before distinguished guests — academics, archivists, curators, members, relations, friends, the Lord Lieutenant of North Yorkshire, patron of the society, Sir Marcus Worsley, Lady Worsley, and Joan's cousin, Lady Ingilby. The president, Dr R M Butler, led the

The ceremony in the rooms of the Yorkshire Archaeological Society, Leeds, in 1994, when the society's Silver Medal was presented to Marie and Joan. (Above) The vice-president Gordon Forster gives the address, with the president, Dr R M Butler, next to him; (below) Marie and Joan respond.

proceedings, and Gordon Forster, vice-president, gave the address. We responded by expressing our thanks, and speaking of our long association with the society as part of our work. Our friends, Peter and Janet Leyland, from Askrigg were guests, and Janet (a well-known artist) took an excellent video of the occasion. The honour crowned our careers.

An unlooked-for marvel of this era was the sudden popularity of Marie's wood engravings. Until Ken Smith published the special editions, they had remained unnoticed for fifty years. An astonishing number had been sold at Ingleton and Leeds, and local galleries also took them up. Then, Rosemary Davidson, the owner of a farmhouse turned into a small art gallery in Arkengarthdale and of Broughton House Gallery in Cambridge, presented a Christmas show at the latter gallery in 1994 of work by Gwen Raverat, Jean Lodge and Marie. Again many were sold. *Multiples*, the newsletter of the Society of Wood-Engravers, noticed the exhibition, saying that 'Marie's engraved scenes of the Yorkshire countryside are truly delightful'. A spin-off was the publication in 1995, as part of a series, of a little book of a selection of the engravings published by the Quince Press at Bury St Edmunds.

A large part of the winter of 1993-94 was spent in compiling and editing a book of Joan's poems. This had been Marie's idea, as she felt that this side of Joan's talents had been neglected. Beautifully produced in hardback, it was published by Smith Settle in December 1994. Many of the poems had been written in the 1930s, and so were dubbed old-fashioned, but others spoke appreciatively of them, and David Morgan Rees in *Yorkshire Journal* wrote: 'These short poems have a simple lyrical quality distilled from gentle, sometimes ironic observation of the world.' *Poems* is a publication which we treasure.

The year 1995 is a winding-up. Beginning in the autumn of 1994, we started to write our reminiscences, *Fifty Years in the Yorkshire Dales*, and finished them in June the following year. The last Christmas reunion of the Askrigg Art Club had taken place in December. At the request of the new editor of the *Dalesman*, we had written a tribute to Phyllis Bentley to celebrate the centenary of her birth. Dick Chapman died in 1981, J B Priestley in 1984, and Lettice Cooper, aged ninety-six, in 1994. In March of that same year Alf Wight, alias James Herriot, died, and his books, and as it so happened those of Hannah Hauxwell, promoted by Barry Cockroft, came to an end. All boosted by television have provided popular entertainment, and no doubt sold far more copies than ours did. No longer as in the 1930s had we had the field to ourselves. It is true that in modern times we had been the first to put the Dales on the map.

However, in 1994 Ken Smith outlined plans for a programme of reprints, including *A Dales Heritage*, *Yorkshire Album* and *A Dales Album* , and a new book of all the Yorkshire Dales wood engravings, not in a limited edition but printed for popular consumption. Other titles are also being discussed for publication. Who can say that we shall not write another book? But 'Time's winged Charriot [is] hurrying near'.

Publications

Swaledale by Ella Pontefract and Marie Hartley (J M Dent, 1934).
Wensleydale by Ella Pontefract and Marie Hartley (J M Dent, 1936).
Wharfedale by Ella Pontefract and Marie Hartley (J M Dent, 1938).
The Charm of Yorkshire Churches by Ella Pontefract and Marie Hartley (*Yorkshire Weekly Post*, 1936).
Yorkshire Tour by Ella Pontefract and Marie Hartley (J M Dent, 1939).
Yorkshire Cottage by Ella Pontefract and Marie Hartley (J M Dent, 1942).
Yorkshire Heritage by Marie Hartley (J M Dent, 1950).
The Old Hand-Knitters of the Dales by Marie Hartley and Joan Ingilby (Dalesman, 1951).
Yorkshire Village by Marie Hartley and Joan Ingilby (J M Dent, 1953).
The Yorkshire Dales by Marie Hartley and Joan Ingilby (J M Dent, 1956).
The Wonders of Yorkshire by Marie Hartley and Joan Ingilby (J M Dent, 1959).
Yorkshire Portraits by Marie Hartley and Joan Ingilby (J M Dent, 1961).
Getting to Know Yorkshire by Marie Hartley and Joan Ingilby (J M Dent, 1964).
Life and Tradition in the Yorkshire Dales by Marie Hartley and Joan Ingilby (J M Dent, 1968).
Life and Tradition in the Moorlands of North- East Yorkshire by Marie Hartley and Joan Ingilby (J M Dent, 1972).
Life and Tradition in West Yorkshire by Marie Hartley and Joan Ingilby (J M Dent, 1976).
A Dales Heritage by Marie Hartley and Joan Ingilby (Dalesman, 1982).
Dales Memories by Marie Hartley and Joan Ingilby (Dalesman, 1986).
Yorkshire Album by Marie Hartley and Joan Ingilby (J M Dent, 1988).
The Yorkshire Dales: wood engravings by Marie Hartley (limited edition, Smith Settle, 1989).
A Dales Album by Marie Hartley and Joan Ingilby (J M Dent, 1991).
Yorkshire Dales Wood Engravings: A Further Selection, by Marie Hartley (Smith Settle, 1991).
Forms and Colours by Marie Hartley (Smith Settle, 1992).
A Favoured Land: Yorkshire in text and image (Smith Settle, 1994).
Poems by Joan Ingilby (Smith Settle, 1994).
Fifty Years in the Yorkshire Dales by Marie Hartley and Joan Ingilby (Smith Settle, 1995).